The Perfect Minister's Wife:

Another Book of Fiction

Joy Keating Gulick

ISBN: 1-4663-8665-7
ISBN-13: 9781466386655

Dedication

This book is dedicated with love and affection to my wonderful, bright husband, Roger, who is a remarkable pastor and very much a part of my story, a story that wouldn't have happened without him.

And to my brother, Paul Keating, whose editing and creativity amazes me and whose brothering has always encouraged me.

CONTENTS

Chapter 1
NO WAY

A minister's wife? Get real.

Live in the South? No way.

But, I confess, since those early, youthful declarations, I've been a minister's wife for a lot of years and my pastor husband and I now live in the South. But I wasn't unusual, for few of us knew about ourselves when we were young, and few knew in advance what God's good plan for our life would be. But, over the years my life as a mostly "Southern" minister's wife has been an incredible, funny, difficult, and life-changing journey—mostly funny. But I've learned many lessons and made many mistakes.

I share my sojourn of God's sometimes scary, often surprising, frequently hilarious sojourn, in order that those of you in a pastor's house who are coming along behind me, will take a deep breath, have a smile and hopefully relax a little bit more in your curious, unique role as The Pastor's Wife.

So get a cup of tea, sit down and enjoy one wife's journey. To start, I never wanted to be what I thought would be a dowdy, old minister's wife; nor did I want to have to live under the watchful eyes of hundreds in a congregation (mostly the women) who would critique me and my family—even though there were probably plenty of things for them to critique. My house would probably never be neat enough and our kids would probably never win prizes for being model children. I also thought I had to be straight-faced, solemn and Miss America perfect. How wrong and naive I was.

As a Northerner, I didn't want to live in the South because…well, because I had lived in the North all my life (it's just that simple) and I *just knew* the customs and behaviors of Northerners were the right ones. The way we did things was comfortable and familiar. On top of that, I never could quite figure out why one had to say, "Yes, 'Ma'am" or "Yes, Sir" to one's parents. How formal! How stilted. What was wrong with, "O.K. Mom?" (Said in a loving voice of course.) How prejudiced I was, and how much I needed to learn.

"I know the plans I have for you, to prosper you, to give you a future and a hope." Jeremiah 29:11.

Chapter 2
WHERE THE JOURNEY BEGAN

Little did I know as I went through my early years of life that God was preparing me for His use in ways I would never have guessed?

After my screaming arrival at 3 a.m. in our family home in Trenton, New Jersey, our father, somewhat disheveled, said to my brothers and sister when he woke them. "Get up, Get up, Hurry! You have a new sister downstairs." No child knew the word pregnant then. There was no such thing. Storks, maybe. "Yea, sure" they groaned and rolled over to get that last wink, assuming it was another of his tricks to get them up for school.

Who would have thought that day in my mother's bedroom, when my eyes squinted open for the first time and five faces looked down at me in my mothers arms that the *Planner of Life* was preparing me for a life of people and ministry. Those five faces were two brothers, a sister and my parents Mary and Joseph. (With parents called Mary and Joseph how could I have done anything but ministry?) Each of those five had their share in shaping me for becoming a minister's wife. As I grew they loved me, called me awful names and assured me that I really was adopted and not wanted. They often kept me from what I wanted to do, scared me, punched me, taught me some very important lessons, and also taught me how to have fun. Now, doesn't that list sound like good preparation experiences for church life?

That was my auspicious beginning in my parent's bedroom with five faces staring down at me, and I have been surrounded with people ever since.

As I grew, I was taught all the Bible stories, of course, all from the King James Version, *(For God so loved the world... and come unto me, etc...)*, and frequently met many missionaries and pastors around our dinner table. My father was the director of an inner-city ministry. It was the 1930's and the Great Depression and many vagrants suffered from alcoholism and no employment. Our frequent clergy and missionary guests all assured me that I was a very cute little girl. Consequently, at an early age I decided those people were so nice and I was so cute that I would be a *Missionary*—and a *Mother*. But I still wasn't sure in which order that was supposed to occur.

At age twelve, and even though the economic realities of the depression were all around, life was good and fun. As a family we laughed a lot and loved our big, old, Victorian house. Hide and seek on a rainy day could go on for hours. We used the pantry closet to play store. The fireplaces warmed the sitting room for our Sunday evening snacks of peanut butter and jelly with the crusts cut off.

But then, for reasons that were never revealed, we moved to a new town, into a, sadly, smaller, ordinary house. I was awkward at my new school and was without friends since I transferred mid-year. In my anxiousness about breaking into a group, any group, I began to compromise *our family's standards.*

When I became a full fledged junior higher, my mantra was that lying and stealing were good, five and ten cent stores were easy shoplifting targets; and sure I began the adventure of smoking cigarettes and trying some wine at a girlfriend's house. "I don't want you hanging around that girl." My first cigarette, a Lucky Strike, was a definite challenge. It tasted awful. My mother threatened to *break both my arms and legs* if I even thought about such sins. I had a hard time getting that first cigarette in my mouth and lit, but I persevered in spite of the threats.

Needless to say, church at that point was dull and boring. At every chance, I would sneak out and go to my friend's house across from the church when I was supposedly in Sunday school. Mother was in the choir—so who would know? I remember, at my most guilty moments—about every third week or so—getting down by my bed and asking God to please forgive me.

One January night when I was fourteen, my older brother invited me to a youth event at the local church he was attending. I was in my best, "I hate church" mode, so I have no idea why I went. As a safeguard, I invited a girlfriend to go with me in case it got too boring. Little did I know that I would have a life changing experience. From the moment the speaker started talking, the Spirit of God was speaking louder. At the end of the service, the minister gave an invitation for me (It seemed I was the only one there.) to give my life to Christ and to be forgiven. I could do no other. The Spirit of God drew me to himself with great, loving warmth. Now, I wanted to follow Christ. I wept as I stood at the front of the church, I felt *washed inside and out* and given a new desire to follow Christ with *my whole being.* That was the way we described it. But whatever the description, I was different. I knew I was forgiven and there welled up in me such an incredible joy. Now I was eager to do what ever He desired. I was a new person.

Two years later, at the same church, (By then I was attending several times a week.) another missionary speaker came. I remember thinking, *I could be a missionary,* if God so desired. My nagging fear, though, was that I was going to be sent to the wildest part of the Amazon jungle, and like any cliché, I would have to live in a tree hut and fight off angry, naked savages. (That was, at least, an interesting teenage fantasy.) But I was willing to go, a little naive perhaps, but willing. At best I wanted to be obedient to His call. **Now that was a good mental attitude for a future pastor's wife in a suburban jungle.**

So, with the encouragement of an uncle, who just happened to be on the Board of Trustees, I applied to Wheaton College. Off I went to college to prepare to be *a missionary*. I secretly laughed at the possibility of getting into Wheaton College which was often referred to as the *Harvard* of Christian schools—surprisingly and happily my application was accepted and I loved my whole time there.

As I reflect back on those college years I am aware that there were important spiritual and personal lessons I needed to come to grips with that would influence how I approached the rest of my years. Many of those lessons were discovered at daily chapel. I heard incredible stories about God's faithfulness, yes, even in those Amazon and heart-of-darkest-African jungles, in Kuala Lumpur and China as well, with its inscrutable people and places. God was present in those esoteric places and was spinning out his purposes in miraculous ways. I left those years at Wheaton with a refreshed and expanded sense of a loving God who is always there and is working his wonderful will in more ways than I could fathom.   When I became a Christian in high school, I had the marvelously immature idea that now I, (emphases on the I) was to do the right thing and be the right person, and witness, and be good (no more cigarettes) and read my Bible every day. At College I discovered that the Holy Sprit was assigned to guide and empower me to do God's will. That was an amazing refreshing discovery. I just needed to be dependent on

God's power to accomplish any task. I didn't need to run around doing things for him, but to be available for Him to do things through me. I spent time before God finding out what He wanted and trusting him to help me do what ever He asked. Of course, knowing is not always doing. He is still working these truths into my life.

As you read this book you will see how God gently, *and not so gently,* worked these truths into my life. Other thoughts I heard in chapel over and over again that impacted me were: "Not somehow, but triumphantly." "It's always too soon to quit." "Never doubt in the darkness what God showed you in the light."[1] (I've drawn on those thoughts frequently). And a thought my father repeated to me every time he wrote or telephoned: "Keep on keeping on." It was made clear through other speakers and classroom professors that the mission field is not just in foreign countries but any place God puts you whether in an American neighborhood, a bank or Iraq. Where God *put me* after graduation was in Baltimore, Maryland on Young Life staff. My first reaction was that Young Life was neither adventurous nor glamorous or overseas. Young Life is a Christian organization that reaches out to non-Christian high school students. However, on staff I very quickly learned to trust God in new ways. I had to raise my own financial support. That was scary. Nevertheless I raised just enough to start, and gloriously callow, I arrived on a Greyhound bus with my tattered luggage in downtown, scary Baltimore.

I was without a car, without an apartment, and without even a bed. All I had was $25 and lots of faith. My new boss must have thought, "What have we hired?" As time went by I discovered that he, Jerry Johnson, was a very fun loving and incredible mentor. My first week on staff Jerry told me there

1   *V. Raymond Edmond, president, Wheaton College, Wheaton, Illinois.*

was a volunteer on staff who had an extra room in her apartment, but no extra bed. She said she would take me in.

So, one afternoon, in that strange town, I took a bus to a shabby shopping mall to buy a bed. I was into missionary 101 and over my head, or so I thought. While bumping along, with a stop at every corner, I prayed: "Please, please, Lord, help me find a bed!" My faith was wavering. What had I gotten myself into?

I thought my best strategy for the first store I went into would be to affect a casual look-around, just "researching" the price of a single bed. "Do you have any cots?" I asked the middle aged man in a rumpled black suit. The clerk smilingly took me to the half empty second floor where he had two sizes of cots—little and littler. I thought that I *should* start with the larger one, (I maybe could turn over on that one.), and anyway I didn't want to look too poor to the salesman.

"This one is $69.00," he volunteered.

Sheepishly I asked, "How 'bout that little one over there?" "$39.00."

"Thank you very much," I said as though I were merely on a fact finding trip for a major decorating firm. I walked away, scribbling in my note book, knowing full well, I had not fooled him.

"Would you like to see the bargain basement?" he graciously called after me. I tried to be indifferent. "Oh, um, ok, yes." We went downstairs and he showed me a bed with a headboard and a box spring. It looked great. But he quickly pointed out a tiny crack in the headboard, but assured me it wouldn't be seen. "How much?" I hated myself for having to be so poor, but I imagined I had carried it off with great Academy Award indifference. "I can let you have the whole thing for $20.00" he said, with just the hint of a smile. I didn't even blink.

I asked casually, (I was in a Hollywood actress mode by now), "Do you deliver?"

"Oh, yes, m'am."

"How much?"

"Oh, we deliver...free." Inside I was jumping up and down at God's incredible, unexpected provision. But the story was not over.

"Do you want delivery today?" He was smiling even broader this time. Wow! I wouldn't be sleeping on the floor my first night as a struggling, very young and inexperienced missionary in Baltimore.

That was my first big lesson in trust and preparations for those lean years in the pastorate. Always trust God, especially when finances are tight.

Chapter 3

AN INVALUABLE BOOT CAMP FOR CHURCH LIFE

"**Y**ou must win the right to be heard" My first hand experience of seeing this truth in action was my first year on Young Life Staff. My boss, Jerry Johnson said, "Joy, I'm going to drop you off at a high school campus today so you can just start getting to know the kids." He pulled the car over to the curb across from a mammoth high school campus. Scary stuff. I had no clue what to do. "Go to it," he cheerily said. "Have fun." I'll pick you up at 4:30. He drove off.

I wondered how in the world this was going to work, and how in the world I was going to *have fun*. After all I was *a college graduate* and there I was walking around a high school campus trying to figure out how I would get to know students. Collecting my wits I discovered that there was a girl's hockey practice going on in the athletic field. I casually strolled over, just to watch, mind you, to try to catch some of the names of the girls. There was someone calling, "Mary, hey Mary, see ya tomorrow," as the girl walked off the field. So at the appropriate moment I said, "Hi, Mary," "That was a great shot." She was probably wondering what kind of creep I was or whose older sister.

The next day I was back again at the hockey field and waited for another chance to say, "Hi, Mary." After two weeks of watching the practices and learning names, the girls finally came up *to me* and asked, "Are you going to be at our out-of-town game?" "Well, yeah...sure, of course." Giggling, they said in unison, "Could you give us a ride?" I almost fell over. God had opened up a door for me to get to know them and love them a little bit. After about a month of *non-intrusive* friendliness, they asked me, "Joy, who *are* you?" I said that I worked with high school students and asked if they would like to come and visit one of our Young Life clubs in a near by high school. Enthusiastically they said, "Yes, we'll be there, sounds cool." It works, I thought to myself. Within six month of my winning the right to be heard, the Young Life *guy leader* and I had a club of thirty-five students from Catonsville High School. As the year wore on a few of the students announced their faith in Christ.

This principle of *Relational Evangelism* proved as effective in our church ministry. The principle is to get involved with people where they live. Show genuine Christian caring and love until they trust you enough and want to know whatever it is that makes you tick. "People don't care how much you know until they know how much you care." Where are the people in your church, and outside your church? Junior League, playing tennis, Newcomers' Club, their kids' school, PTA? Are they at the country club, swimming pool, block parties, the grocery store? Our role model is Christ. Christ went where the people were. Likewise as pastors' wives we need to enter their world to get to know them so we can love them, care for them and eventually have them become captivated by Christ's love. It's exciting, but not always a one, two, three instant event.

One of the churches Roger pastored was in a rather wealthy neighborhood. The country club gave all pastors' families free memberships to *The Club*. I was fortunate to spend many a summer taking my kids to the club's pool. I sat at the side of the pool and talked to the other young mothers. What doors *that* opened for future ministry. We found that when we were going to the events at the club, our ministry at the church and in the community was so much more effective. Somehow, because we entered *their* world they sensed that we cared and they were more comfortable around us and open to what we had to say. It was very incarnational. In Hebrews 4:14 it shows the importance of this principle of entering peoples' worlds. *"Therefore, since we have a great high priest who has gone through the heavens, Jesus the Son of God, let us hold firmly to the faith we profess. For we do not have a high priest who is unable to sympathize with our weaknesses, but we have one who has been tempted in everyway, just as we are, yet was without sin. Let us then approach the throne of grace with confidence so that we may receive mercy and find grace to help us in our time of need."* Christ came through the heavens to where we were and lived. So we also need to enter the world of those to whom we are ministering.

I came from a heritage that said, "Come out from among them and be ye separate." Which was interpreted, "Don't go where non-Christians go or where non-Christian activities are going on." What was conveniently skipped over in those old days were the stories about Christ talking to the woman at the well, possibly a prostitute, or Jesus going to the house of a tax collector who was the most hated person in the neighborhood. *Separate,* obviously means we are not to participate in the sin, but not to withdraw into a cloister either. What a delight it was to see God transform people's lives through simple acts of entering their world and loving them. It takes time, but God is the lord of time.

"Jesus does not stand before the blind and leper and the poor and the sinner and discourse philosophically on why they are in such

a condition, but lays his hands of sympathy upon them and heals them thru His servants." E. Stanley Jones- India 1884-1973.

Chapter 4
THE REST IS HISTORY

I was driving to Baltimore from the Colorado Young Life Ranch, where I had worked that summer, when the impulse to go see my family in New Jersey flashed into my head. I can do it, why not? I had time off from my job and I was at the right exit to easily get there. Little did I know that God had a life changing encounter waiting for me.

I hugged Mom as we shared all of our catch up news. She told me that my older brother was there as well, and that he had brought a friend. At that Paul walked in followed by a tall, handsome man I'd never seen before. I thought, "Now, he's cute." Young Mr. Cute, it turned out, was an officer in the Navy and about to be shipped out from his base at the Philadelphia Navy Yard. Well, so much for that brief encounter.

Typically, I would visit Philadelphia every couple of weeks to visit my brother, who had just returned from a short missionary trip to Africa. Roger, that young Navy officer, it seemed, was always at Paul's. Naturally, being the shy and retiring type, I turned on my best charm offensive. It must have worked...ever so slowly. Months later, to my surprise Roger asked me to go on a church sponsored ski weekend. Of course I went.

I fell in love on the beginner's slope, and on the nighttime ice skating rink and on the ski lifts, and under the snow covered lanterns that dimly lit the walkways. Surprise, surprise, we discovered that we both had a heart for ministry and lots and lots of common interests. Roger told me he had three more years in the Navy and then was planning to go to Seminary in order to do college work with Inter-Varsity Christian Fellowship (a college ministry on secular campuses). Seminary? I wasn't so sure about that.

Eight months later and after amazingly few dates between his cruises and my graduate school and Young Life career, Roger finally, very romantically, asked me to marry him. We were aboard his ship and as we gazed out a porthole Roger surprised me with a beautiful diamond ring. I forget whether he did the on-one-knee ritual but my answer was, "Yes, of course, yes. Yes. I love you."

Six month later, after Roger returned from a cruise in Aleutian Islands, we were married and I was an officer's wife in a brand new world! I totally loved it. While Roger was at sea I moved to New Hampshire and was able to get a job as a teacher of fourth graders. It was a wonderful chance to save some money for Roger's years in seminary.

The pastorate never entered my mind because Inter-Varsity staff was our goal. Well, we discovered God had other plans. Some of which were hilarious, some bewildering, but all are shared with you on our unique adventure.

Chapter 5
STRANGE GUIDANCE

It's never like you think it's going to be. Guidance that is. We thought we had our life all scheduled. Roger was going to seminary in order to go on Inter Varsity staff. He came to faith in Christ through Inter-Varsity at the University of Illinois and they mentored him. He became the president of the I-V Chapter and led a Bible study in his fraternity. He seemed to be made for college student work and with his gift mix he was a shoo in for staff. We found ourselves in Southern California at Fuller Seminary and it was his senior year.

Roger being disciplined and responsible had that application for I-V staff in early. Then a fork in the road popped into our lives. We got a letter from my best girlfriends' husband asking Roger to be his associate pastor in Salisbury, Maryland. We knew the answer. No! Inter Varsity was our choice. Roger had been on associate I-V staff at California State College in Los Angeles and worked with International students also while in seminary, so our hearts were set. But we didn't hear from Inter-Varsity and the pastor from Maryland gave us a deadline in March to give him an answer. We began saying, "Lord, we need to make a decision about this church. They need an answer and we are pretty sure it's no. Please show us." We still didn't hear from Inter-Varsity. That seemed so strange. As an unprejudiced wife, I knew Roger would be accepted on campus staff, but time clicked on and still no answer. We came to the decision deadline for the church job. We prayed and Roger began to think that working in a college town as an associate pastor with college students and high school students and young adults might really be a good challenge. We said yes.

Some time later we heard that Roger's application for Inter Varsity had slipped down the back of a filing cabinet and got lost. Hmm. God works in strange and wonderful ways. As we look back we are very grateful we were directed to church ministry. So when you are in the fog of decision making about what church or what ministry, know that God has not forgotten about you. He is always there directing your path.

"Trust in the Lord with all your heart and lean not on your own understanding. In all your ways acknowledge Him and He will direct your path."

Chapter 6
DID WE MAKE A MISTAKE?

There are times in the pastorate that can be difficult, *very* difficult indeed, but often life-changing as well. Through the difficult times Romans 8:28, *"All things work together for good for those who love Him,"* becomes a reality.

It was our first church; Roger was the associate pastor working with youth and young adults and preaching once a month. Like so many 300 year old northeastern churches, the general mood was rather funereal. Not much spiritually was going on in the lives of the members. We wondered, like Elijah, if there were *any* real Christians in the town; if there were, we hadn't run into them. (That was a naïve sense of things at the time, but was our true feelings.) After we had been at the church for two grinding, uneventful years, I started to notice that Roger seemed a bit depressed, not his normal self. As we talked one morning, he said he was thinking about leaving the ministry. "Nothing's happening in the lives of these people through my ministry. *Maybe I'm not really called to ministry.* Look at the facts. There were about six kids in the youth group, and the young adults seem totally disinterested in Bible studies or small groups of any kind. He said that he wasn't sure that he wanted to push on.

Roger, on the advice of a friend, decided to go to Princeton for occupational testing to see if he was better fitted for some other career. Thinking of myself and my loss of identity,

I didn't like that suggestion. However, in his undergraduate days Roger had received his degrees in mathematics. "Maybe I'd be more effective as a lay person. Also I can do a mean pi squared, even a two plus two," he said without smiling. If I speak to them about Christ as just a regular person instead of a pastor, it might catch them off guard and they might listen more carefully.

So off we went to Princeton for vocational and psychological testing and evaluation. A wife is a part of the dynamics of any clergyman, so we were off together. After the tests, a psychologist suggested that perhaps working in a place like IBM or at a theological library would be more of Roger's natural bent. As I participated in the in-depth evaluation interviews, a sense of sadness came over me. Hadn't Roger done well in seminary and enjoyed and been effective in ministry until now? He was too young for a mid-life crisis. Anyway, in my imagination, a life with IBM didn't sound so good. And more importantly, in my most important, altruistic self, I wondered what would become of *me*? I'd been involved with Roger in the youth work and a small group. We would have separate careers. Reluctantly, I knew that if this was what God wanted, it would be good—it *would* be good, wouldn't it? But my emotions hadn't caught up with that idea yet.

Roger applied for a job with IBM and passed the tests with flying colors. (Even though they weren't my favorite colors.) He spent a day in the IBM office and said he felt at home there and knew he could do well. The great, grey corporation offered him a job—with a great salary. (Well, maybe I needed to rethink this whole thing. Hmm.)

A short time later, back home, Roger was reading the scriptures in his quiet time; he read about Peter's activities after Christ's death. Peter went back to his fishing nets, his old job, and his comfort zone where he had been a successful professional. Strange though, he wasn't catching any fish.

Then Jesus strolled by on the shore and said the familiar words, "Peter," Raising his voice, "Hey Peter, just throw those nets on the other side of the boat." Peter thought that was one of the dumber things he had heard, but, OK, he'd indulge whomever it was shouting at him through the fog. We all know the story; dozens of fish filled his nets.

Roger knew he was comfortable with mathematics and computers; after all he had been an honor student in those fields. Like Peter and his fishing trade, going to IBM for Roger would be doing what he knew best. It would be very comfortable. But was God saying: Roger, put *your* nets down again and we'll see what we can do in your church. "OK, Lord, if you want me to continue in ministry, help me to lead someone to Christ—this week."

Now that was a risky challenge. And seven days later (So often it seems to be at the last minute.), Roger had lunch with Harry an engineer with whom he'd spent some time. He was trying to get to know Harry better and hopefully build a bridge to talk with him about his faith. After a good lunch of a crab salad sandwich, some iced tea and talk about sports, jobs and families, Harry, all of a sudden, had some questions about God and science. After all, he *was* talking to a clergyman whom he had come to trust. What's wrong with talking about God? Finally after exploring Harry's concerns, God and science, contradictions, Roger asked the question, "Harry, are you really concerned about these questions, or are you just trying to keep God at arm's length?" Tears welled in Harry's eyes as he said, "You nailed me, I am trying to keep God away." They walked to the church and knelt down in the sanctuary. Harry committed his life and will to Christ. Roger prayed a prayer of thanks.

The same week two high school girls in our youth group asked me about Young Life Ranches. They had heard about them and wanted to go; after all, who wouldn't want to go to Colorado where all the cute guys are? At the week-long camp they became Christians, returned home and begged us to start a Young Life Club. It just so happened that the two girls who had gone to the ranch were about the two most popular girls in their school. So when they invited people to a new club, they all would all show up. So they invited 50 kids and 49 showed up for our first get-together. From there, the club's numbers went to eighty and then to 100. Word spread quickly. That was the beginning of an outpouring of God's Spirit on the whole congregation and then the town.

The nets had been lowered on the other side of the boat and God had filled them. Roger refers to that time as his second calling to the ministry. We recognized again that it wasn't his abilities, his talents or his intellect, but his availability to God's power. Sadly, we both had to learn from God's lesson book, over and over again, as we faced our new ministry disappointments and triumphs.

"There is no situation so chaotic that God cannot, from that situation, create something that is surprisingly good. He did it at creation; He did it at the cross. He is doing it today." Bishop Moule.

Chapter 7
MISCALCULATION

Laugh with me, it will give you the courage to laugh when similar situations happen to you. Most times it's laughing. Sometimes it's tears.

Our second church assignment came about when we were invited by phone to the mountains of Tennessee. George, the senior minister, wanted us to candidate for an assistant pastor position. Roger, when asked to consider this position, said, "I don't really think I'm called to mountain missions."

However, the wise senior pastor warmly and knowingly suggested, "Well, why don't you just come along for a few days and just take a look at us folks here and meet some of the people. We'll cover your expenses." Trying to be open to whatever God had for us, Roger decided to at least look the situation over; also because a short time earlier he had written out what he thought would be the perfect job description for him and it was pretty close to what the pastor showed him.

The pastor, a former Air Force pilot, flew us to Chattanooga in his plane. We got in his car and began driving up the twisty, steep road to the top of the mountain. The houses we then passed, those that we could see through the tall trees, kept getting bigger and bigger and incredibly more beautiful. They were all surrounded by "White House-huge" lawns with gates of iron and stone. "Umm, Roger," I slowly said as I was awed from looking out the car window, "I wonder if we brought the right clothes."

We discovered much to our chagrin, that the mountain was one of the wealthiest suburbs in Tennessee-so much for our *mountain missions'* fantasy.

We arrived at what looked like a Gothic cathedral with a vaulted sanctuary ceiling and magnificent rose windows. We had instantly liked the handsome senior pastor who then graciously showed us around the church with its beautifully appointed rooms. We were most impressed by the quality of this man and his wife. They were godly, fun, and soon to be discovered, "full of integrity."

When the subject turned to where we would live we were introduced to a woman dressed in a top–of-the-line, casual dress. I remember thinking how elegant and pretty she was. She enthusiastically told us, with her creamy southern accent, "Honey, we have in our church a lovely woman, you'll just love her. She owns an extra house and wants to give it to the church to use as a manse for the new assistant pastor. She calls the house: "Number 10 Downing Street."

After seeing the proposed manse nestled in the woods with a little creek running behind it, I thought, "Oh, this could be good, good, *good*." But is this where we are supposed to be?

We went back home and thought and prayed for two weeks. After wrestling with the decision (Wrestling because we loved the youth and young adults we worked with so very much.), we said, "Yes" to the new church. We would go. The yes was made some what easier because the job description fit Roger so well.

Everything back home was bleak and colorless as we began to put our worldly belongings into packing boxes. A week later, the owner of our supposed new manse called and said, "I was thinking that if it would be all right with y'all, I'd like to turn 10 Downing Street's garage into a twenty by twenty foot room."

I said, being unaware of her Southern cadence, "The house is really just fine as is." "Do you want an extra bedroom or a den?" she asked.

Not having a clue what I was doing, I said, "May we think about it for a couple of days?" Roger and I decided that a bedroom for guests would probably be best. I telephoned to tell her of our decision.

"Oh, my dear, I'm so embarrassed. We've already begun the den." That's when we discovered that Mrs. West was a wonderful, generous, warm person; but when she had made up her mind, that was that. As it turned out, we practically lived in that den, our kids and dog loved it, along with hundreds of high school students, kids in junior high and young adult small groups always crowded the room. We wouldn't have had a place sufficient for our lifestyle if she hadn't smoothly made a better choice.

Then Mrs. West telephoned me at our former church home and said she wanted to fly me to Chattanooga so that I could pick out paint colors, carpets, *chandeliers!* My stomach cramped. *What price range should I choose? What if she doesn't like my choices?* It was her house we were decorating. I never had such carte blanche to be a decorating wizard before. Yes, people have told me that I have a flair for decorating, but what if Danny (she insisted I call her by the name all her *friends* called her) didn't agree? She said she would fly me in to make whatever choices I wanted. I wondered what we'd gotten ourselves into.

When I arrived at the airport, Danny met me and took me to her home for lunch. (Didn't anyone know I was the little, simple girl from New Jersey?) We sat in front of a huge crackling fireplace while a charming maid was shuttling in and out of the kitchen to meet our every whim. I don't think I fooled Danny into thinking that all this gracious, southern hospitality was normal for me. But it was fun.

When we went shopping, I was told I could have picked out anything I wanted for our manse, but thoughtfully, or so I thought, I tried to pick the medium price. "What color shall we paint the den, Joy?" Little did she know that the den we were moving from was about 9 by 6, and the only color was a tattered, drab, gold, corduroy day-bed we had bought at a yard sale. Our only other *grand* piece of furniture was a small wooden rocking chair. It was no antique from my great grandmother's attic, mind you, but a friend's cast-off. And of course we had a basic 12 inch TV.

"A soft gold would be nice." I said.

A month later we arrived at Lookout Mountain in our stuffed, aging car, with two, not very enthusiastic kids. We were to stay the first night at a lovely motel on the mountain until the moving van arrived the next day. Fresh garden flowers had been placed in the room by a thoughtful church member. "That's just the way we like to do things here, honey."

Of course we were eager to see the manse and all that had been done. We went with the senior pastor's wife to see our new home. There were several ladies carefully manicuring the lawn and the geranium-laden flower boxes. The new den that had been added was right out of *Southern Living.* The wood paneling had been bleached and stained a soft gold. The new gold carpet was chosen to harmonize.

Wide eyed, I walked into the freshly painted kitchen; on the counter was a French country basket, laden with fresh fruit with miniature, green leaves and flowers tucked into the spaces between the fruit. I opened the new refrigerator; it too was brimming with ham, a turkey, cokes, recently baked bread, salads, and a homemade, chocolate cake. Certainly *Gourmet Magazine* would be by tomorrow to do a special spread, I was sure. Do you think they might have forgotten the ice cream in the freezer?

The soaps in the bathroom, of course, matched the wall paper and toilet tissue. Every room was completely re-done: new carpets and paint and creative wallpaper every-where. There were white shutters at each window. We could barely take it all in. Eat your heart out.

There was just one little problem. Our truckload of furniture was about to arrive. And as I've said, it was all es-pecially selected early Salvation Army and hand-me-downs.

That night Roger and I lay in bed at the motel. I couldn't sleep. I was worrying about what Danny would think when she saw all our forlorn poor pastor's junk placed in her perfect little house. We didn't sleep. At two in the morning I said, "Roger, let's put that red sewing machine table that we thought was so clever, in the attic."

At four o'clock Roger said, "Let's put everything in the attic!" We started to laugh and couldn't get stopped. There were tears of hilarious anxiety.

In the morning the moving truck arrived and unloaded our dreary, earthly treasures. Could Danny be far behind? I dreaded the moment.

In the midst of my dread, the senior pastor's wife and her friends showed up to help. They generously (maybe sym-pathetically) saw the situation and began running to their attics to find something that would rescue our pathetic situa-tion. My stomach was in a bigger knot. We had no furniture for the den! One of my rescuers, who easily became my best friend, heard that a church member had a very nice sofa out on the curb in front of her house. It was being sent to the Sal-vation Army. As far as I could tell when they brought it in, it looked perfectly new. With a very serious face, the neighbor/couch owner said with a big smile that she was willing to sell the couch to the new minister's wife for a dollar. *Yes, yes, we'll take it.* It was beautiful.

We all realized in a moment that Danny should not see our old wreck of a couch now in the den. We began moving it (why did I think we should ever bring it in the first place?), but it became wedged between the den and the dining room door.

Someone shouted, "Danny's walking up the drive way." If I could have disappeared I would have. Graciously and slowly Danny came in, said "Mornin'" She walked elegantly through the house, touching each piece of furniture as she went. At the end of her tour she turned and looked at me and said, "Honey, y'all have lots of time."

How kind she was and how relieved I was that that moment was over. The best part was that we became good friends.

For two whole weeks groups of women (the word had gone throughout the church) kept bringing in beautiful things from their attics. How good they were and how faithfully the Lord was in supplying our needs. It was, it turned out, to be one of our best memories of beginning a new ministry. We have laughed so many times about our thinking we were not called to *mountain mission*. We and our mountain friends still laugh hysterically every time I recount the episode.

A good thing to remember is that every church does it differently. This particular church was a feast, but it can be famine. For example: when my husband was in seminary one of the women's groups had talked about the fact that sometimes churches will bring food for you when you move into a church. I thought how nice. Well, at our first church we arrived in our little apartment and I thought to myself, "I wonder if there will be anything in the kitchen." I immediately went to the refrigerator to see if someone had left little goodies, but it was empty. Then being a positive person, I thought I bet they put things in our cupboard. NOPE! If a church is gracious enough to go an extra mile, be very grateful, it is a wonderful but unnecessary gift. I have seen some wives get angry because a church did not do anything for their arrival. That attitude can really get you into trouble. It is an attitude of "They owe me something". They really don't owe us anything. But it sure is nice when it happens.

As the apostle Paul said, *"...for I have learned the secret of contentment in every situation, whether it be...plenty or want..."* Philippians 4:11 (paraphrase).

Chapter 8
WE KNOW HOW

Roger and I moved to our second church. Previously we had what we easily concluded was a successful youth ministry- up to a hundred at a Young Life Club, often more than that when we had a weekend coffee house. And people were regularly coming to faith in Christ. So Roger and I confidently took over the youth ministry in our new town on the mountain. We knew how to do youth work! Just ask us. However, after six months of our magnificent efforts, things were not going so well with our senior high group. (And I'm being charitable in the telling.) Those southern kids were just different. They were polite and all, but I wasn't so sure what their problem was with us Yankees. I was beginning to feel resentment towards them because they were not making us look or feel very successful. After all we were *professionals*. We know how to do youth work. Didn't those kids with their "y'all" accents know that we were doing things right— by the book? They just needed to get with the program (our program).

One morning I told the Lord that I was being bugged by those kids. I had never had such negative feelings for people before. I didn't like those kids now, not one bit. I became a little teary. A whisper floated through my head, "Do you think you were the ones who made your work successful? I hate to tell you this but I was the One who gave you success when you trusted me. Remember how pathetic (I'm sure that was His word.) your work was with only six kids attending? Remember how Roger almost quit the ministry because of his discouragement?

I *had* forgotten.

I confessed to the Lord that I had forgotten who made our work successful, and how self centered my attitude had been. I asked for forgiveness.

My new prayer became, "Lord, help me to love these kids in our youth group no matter what happens, big or little. And give us the wisdom to know what will impact them for Christ. Actually, Lord, John's a pretty nice kid and given a break, Bethany is kinda' cute and even becoming helpful." I rediscovered that it is my continual dependence on the Lord for wisdom and direction and success (or no success) that is needed so I can accomplish what He desires. And that always brings *Him* Glory.

"Not by might, nor by power, but by my spirit says the Lord"

Chapter 9
EARLY WARNINGS

Danny, the lady who gave our manse to the church, asked me before we moved into our new home, if we had a dog. I assured her we didn't. She said, "Good". Two week later one of our college students from our former church came to visit carrying a dog cage with a cute little redbone coonhound puppy. He was so cute and our children were so happy. But I immediately remembered Danny's question. "You don't have a dog do you?" What was I going to do? A friend brought a gift of a puppy and the lady who gave our house to the church clearly did not want a dog in our house. I cautiously called Danny and told her what happened. Her response was somewhat comforting. She said, "O well!?"

You will hear many escapades about this dog, but one of the funnier ones happened a few years later on a beautiful spring day. One of the biggest weddings in the church was taking place and, of course, I was invited since my husband was involved in their marriage ceremony. It was a warm spring day so the church doors were open. I was sitting in the third row of this cathedral like church of slate floors and stone walls and long center aisle. About mid-way through the wedding service, I heard the jingle of our dog's collar. I knew the sound well. Often the dog would jump through the screens in our front door in order to be with us. I started praying. "Oh, Lord, don't let the dog come into the church." I was terrified. He didn't come in. I was so grateful, but as

I stepped out the door after the wedding, my nine year old son came running up to me and said, "Mom, the dog ate the wedding cake!"

I was horrified, and asked, "Where is the dog? Go get him and take him home." I didn't want anyone to know my dog had eaten the cake. I ran to the fellowship hall where the reception was to take place expecting to see crumbs on the plate. No crumbs, but a big bite had been taken out of the cake. I anxiously got a knife and started moving the icing from the sides into the big hole before any one knew the better. Within minutes the cake looked like new, but someone in the wedding party had a mouthful of icing. That day I made plans to join the French Foreign Legion.

Chapter 10
UP TO MY NECK IN TROUBLE

I'm going to tell you two more stories to emphasize the fact that whatever crazy things happen in your church life, I probably did worse and survived to tell, with my friendships intact and a new ability to laugh at my self and not take myself too seriously.

These were the years in the seventies when, where we lived, anyway, you wore long dresses to almost any social event including dinners in homes, weddings, even long casual dresses for casual events. Wigs were also popular for those pool parties where your hair might get all wet and you had to have a quick fix. This particular night the occasion was another one of those incredible pre-wedding parties. I was dressed in one of my particularly nice long party dresses for a pool side catered dinner. I also had a wig on since I had been swimming with my children all day and it was my quick fix. All the waiters had on those short red jackets with trays held high in their hands to bring their goodies to the people mingling at the pool.

It was a beautiful night and anybody who was anybody was there and of course being the minister's wife, we were included in the event. We knew the family well. At about dusk Harry, the teenaged brother of the groom, and I were talking and wondered whether the pool was heated. So we proceeded to walk to the pool to reach down and feel the water. The next thing I know, I was in the deep end of the pool. To this day I have no idea how I got there. Harry was standing at the edge of the pool with his hands in the air saying, "I didn't do it." I looked to my husband hoping he could do something to make everything better, but he was staring at me with disbelief, and never moved. I think I heard him say, "Who is that woman I don't know in the pool?"

The whole group was now staring at me in horror and shock. At this moment I was laughing and crying out of shock and embarrassment. So much for sophistication. No one was coming to my aid. I finally started swimming down to the steps in the shallow end. I thought to myself that I should start doing an Esther Williams, a 1950's movie star swimmer, back stroke with a rose in my mouth. But I quickly thought better of that idea. The hostess of the party graciously met me at the steps and walked me to the tub in her pool dressing room. I stepped into the tub and took off my gown. While standing there alone I shed a few tears with intermingled laughter more from the shock of the whole thing. My wig, by the way, never moved. Thank you Lord!

She brought me this beautiful silk bathrobe to put on, which looked better than my gown. Moments later I walked outside and continued on with the party. Everyone at this point had gotten over the shock and were laughing and comparing it with the night Jacqueline Kennedy fell in to a pool (I think, from being a little drunk.) I have never lived that night down. People still ask me to tell this story.

Chapter 11
OOPS, MY SLIP

A young friend of ours had been in our college student group and was now marrying a pretty, young girl from Memphis. The groom and his prominent family were going to fly us in for the weekend. I packed my long gown and other necessities and off we went. The day of the wedding I realized I hadn't brought my long half slip, but only my short one. That would have been all right, ordinarily, but my summer gown was very sheer. I asked Roger if I had time to buy a long slip. "No, we have to go right away to make it in time for the photographer." My brain was working at full speed, frantically trying to think what I could do. Maybe I could pull the half slip down a little on my hips and it would look half way decent. (There were no safety pins or time to buy them.) I did that and we were off for the wedding.

Roger dashed off for pictures and to get into his robe. I waited for an usher. I was escorted to the third row as part of the family. But as I smilingly walked down the aisle each step my half slip moved slowly down my hips. I surreptitiously put my hand at my hip so nothing would drop to the floor. As I walked, my arm looked paralyzed. As I slid into the designated pew, my demented slip quietly slid to the floor. Looking straight ahead I stepped out of the slip and unseen kicked it under the pew. But how was I going to get out of the church.

After the ceremony, I remained in the pew having decided to wait until everyone had gone. Friends came and chatted with me about the usual, "Wasn't the bride just beautiful?" I stood transfixed in my place, smiling amiably until Roger, finally, came from the pulpit.

I surreptitiously whispered. "Roger, do you see what's on the floor" He looked and said, "What is that?" I quietly whispered, "My slip; lean down and slide it into the sleeve of your clerical robe. Then let's walk toward the front of the church away from the crowd. Walk behind me so no one will see through my dress." We found a room to quickly repair the situation and continue with the party. I just acted like there wasn't light shinning through the skirt of my long dress from my knees down. Maybe no one noticed. Phew, another of Roger's rescues.

Chapter 12
A GOOD LUCK CHARM

Don't be surprised or amazed at what thoughts people have about us minister's wives. One example:

Tennis became one of the sports I had to learn in order to "go where our church people are," or to reach out to those who were not involved in any church. I came to love the game after I learned to hit the ball and became a little proficient. No Serena Williams, mind you, but I could usually get the ball over the net. At our church on the mountain, all the young couples my age played tennis. That was to become our mission field as couples' tennis was the big pastime. The court wasn't the "heart of darkest Africa" with wild angry natives, but husbands and wives, after a tennis fault, were deciding on a no contest divorce and possibly killing each other before the game was over. "If you tell me one more time how to play this game, I'll walk off the court!" In the midst of all those hysterical interactions (certainly *not* between Roger and me) I became a little more proficient at the game.

At our next church, tennis was also *the game*, so I was set. Trudy, a new Christian, asked if I would play in a doubles tournament with her. "Sure, but I'm not very good," I said humbly, actually hoping we might do well. So Trudy (smart lady) decided to pay for us to have some lessons from a tennis pro. That did improve Trudy's and my game a bit. Maybe, maybe, we wouldn't be embarrassed by my playing. We prayed before the big game: "Help us be good sports, and reflect Christ in our attitudes...and help us win!"

I would like to say: we came, we played, we conquered, but no. We lost. This young, new Christian asked: "Why do you think we lost? I thought, for sure, we would win because you were the minister's wife. Why do you think He let us loose?" Trudy, new in her experience with God, was bewildered.

With a smile and a hug, I replied, "They won because they were better."

"Oh." We giggled off the court.

Chapter 13
REAL SUCCESS

Roger and I agreed: if we are successful with our church and fail with our children, something would be wrong. Timothy and Kathleen were our most important congregation, given to us by God. (Of course, we were not always sure about what God had in mind. Nor will you.) How does one juggle ministry and still have time to love one's kids. We decided, up front, to be intentional about our children's spiritual development, and in spite of a busy church schedule, spend quality time with them. We quickly discovered that quality time only appears when we spend quantity time with our children. You and I know parents who have been what seems like stars at parenting but still their children get off the path, way off. In spite of that, we decided, in spite of a busy church schedule, to seek to spend intentional quantity and quality time with them. We were going to take all the steps we could to affirm and build love for God into our children.

After all, as a Christian Education major, I knew that *the home* was where Christian Education should really happen. So Roger and I tried to create fun ways to get God's Word built into their day to day experience.

Fix these words of mine in your hearts and minds. Tie them as symbols on your hands and bind them on your foreheads. Teach them to your children, talking about them when you sit at home and when you walk along the road, when you lie down and when you get up. Write them on the door frames of your houses and on your gate, so that your days and the day of your children may be many...Deut.

11:19-21. Happily we had the help of right-on-target Sunday schools, youth groups and summer camps.

Here are some of the things we worked on—it was always a work in progress:

At breakfast we would have a *short,* child appropriate, devotional that was interactive. We would ask if anyone had a prayer request for that day: tests, friendship issues, feelings, unfinished or unresolved concerns. As we read the scriptures, we didn't insist they sit with their hands folded—not moving. We would read a Bible story or a chapter in *The Narnia Chronicles* while we were eating. (That was probably not according to Ms. Post, but it was according to Ms. Joy.) What that did, we felt, was to let them know that the Word of God was very important in our family. That was an important point for them to get.

Sometimes we even sang *Jesus Loves Me,* or *Make Me a Sunbeam.* (You don't know that one? Get with the 50's. What's your favorite?) It was important to be consistent, like breathing. When I was young, unfortunately, our family got together for devotions very erratically, and sure enough, our father always wanted to be super spiritual when I was in a hurry to get to an event. Yes, that built resentment.

As Tim and Kathy became nine and eleven, we began to have them memorize an age appropriate Bible verse each week. I sometimes paid them to memorize. Pedagogically questionable, perhaps, but **it worked**. Nine and eleven year olds seldom have difficulty memorizing. They can memorize a whole biblical chapter with little difficulty.

There was a chart with each child's name on it, and a space for a star when they had memorized a verse. As one of our pastors said: *Lay up kindling wood in your child's life, and when the match of conversion strikes, the fire will have plenty of fuel.* I found that true in my own life. When I came to faith in Christ at thirteen, I had many verses laid up in my life which

I had memorized as a child. They were there to help me personally and when talking to others of Christ.

At our children's bedtime we always asked the same question: *What was the best thing that happened to you today?* If they didn't have at least one good thing, the *penalty* was that they would have to give us a quarter. I can think of only one time when they had to give up a quarter from their allowance. We asked this question to get them used to being thankful and to get them to share a bit of their lives with us. We hoped this would end each child's day on a happy note. Then Roger or I would pray with each child separately. They loved it. They had their parents' totally focused attention. Also when the "cave" years, early teen years, came on and they just grunted at us through the day, at bed time we would still have these little conversations.

On Sunday afternoons, particularly during those late childhood years, we tried to do something special together: we walked along or in the creeks at the back of the mountain where we were living, (You can do something like this whether you live in downtown Manhattan or Boise, Idaho). We pointed out all the things God created. We examined them and were amazed together at the intricacies and beauty of God's creation. There were flying and nesting birds of every color (or so it seemed), scampering squirrels, awesome, flaming bushes, (Moses would be impressed) filled with red berries. Then, maybe best of all, we would end summer afternoons with a sundae or banana split. (The idea I got from Ruth Graham, Billy's wife.) I think that added a few inches to the waistline...well, forget that. We always tried to put our spiritual times of growth in the context of love and fun.

Importantly, we also often read at dinner some of the books like "The Narnia Chronicles" and "A Wrinkle in Time". They loved being read to..

We only allowed them to watch one hour of television a day, and each day they took turns picking their favorite, wholesome TV show. We wanted them to play outside, get healthy exercise and become creative in their play. They usually watched their hour of TV while I was cooking dinner, which really helped me.

In junior and senior high school, we always sent them to youth group and Sunday school, just like we sent them to school every day. Often parents say, "Our children don't like the youth group. They don't know anyone." Then they let them stay home. "I don't want to force them to go. They may become turned off to God. Interestingly, parents would never allow their children *not* to go to school. They don't fear that they will get turned off to education. But, for some reason, the more important influence of Sunday school or a vital, exciting youth group is allowed to be skipped. We have noticed with other families, where it is a must to go to youth group, the kids usually make friends after they have attended regularly. Sad to say, some youth groups are awful and not worth attending. Then find another group somewhere. Or help make the one you have good.

I always say to moms: "In the summer send your kids to a Christian camp, particularly during junior high and high school. During those years children naturally are separating from parental authority *(Isn't that a nice way to say rebellious?)*, therefore it is important to have other people teaching them about Christ and being with Christian peers. In the summer we sent both our children several times to Teen Missions. Teen Missions is an eight week mission trip to various countries, Mexico, Germany, and Venezuela for instance. There they would participate by building a building, or making a runway for missionary airplanes. They loved it. Plus they were in a safe environment with lots of teens experiencing another world of need, while at the same time growing in

Christ. We also sent them to church camps and Wheaton College's Honey Rock Camp. Those positive experiences helped get them—and us—through their difficult, at least challenging, teen years. On top of that they learned skills like sailing, kayaking, horse back riding, canoeing, and tennis etc.

Recently I asked our now forty-something children if they ever felt as if they lived in a fish bowl as pastor's children? Surprisingly they said, "No." That may be the result of our never saying, "Don't do that; don't do that either" because "what will the people in the church think!" We always tried to base what they did or didn't do on "What would God think?" or "What would we think?" Generally, our kids in their developmental years, were pretty good, but, of course, there were their teen moments when I would have liked to have said those words, but I didn't want them to hate the church or the people in it. Also we should not make our children do or not do something because it would embarrass us, but to do something because it was the right thing to do.

We soon discovered that a very important principle to impart to our children was learning how to ask for *forgiveness.* We modeled it for them, (as best we could, since we were still learning about parenting.) and then we tried to help them learn how to ask for forgiveness from others. We used as a model something like this: *I know I hurt you by* (state the offense). *I am so sorry; would you please forgive me?* No excuses, no reasons for the offense, just a simple admission of doing something hurtful. The person may or may not give forgiveness, but they have done what they could by asking for forgiveness.

One morning Roger was really upset at something Tim did. He jumped all over him, *more than was needed* or appropriate—balance crime to punishment, *to coin a phrase.* Tim went off glumly to school. Roger was feeling uncomfortably guilty while sitting in his office *at the church*; he knew he needed to ask forgiveness from Tim. He didn't want the whole day to go by with Tim feeling badly about himself. He hadn't done anything that bad. Roger walked over to the school and asked the principal, whom he knew, if he could talk to Tim for a moment.

"Of course, Reverend Gulick." When Tim, who was in the fifth grade at the time, curiously came into the office, Roger hugged him, got down on his knees to look at him face to face and then asked Tim if he would forgive him for the way he treated him.

Tim never forgot that moment. Years later he shared that childhood moment in one of his seminary classes. The professor said in an unbelieving voice; "Please tell me that that is a true story!"

Tim answered with some feeling, "Yes, of course," then humorously quipped, "I should lie to my ethics professor?" Not long ago I heard on the radio that professor share that story.

In our children's teen years we put up a poster on their wall. It had a picture of a stream with water rushing over big boulders. Underneath the picture were the words: "With moral principles, stand as a rock: with culture or fashions *go with the flow*." In our kids' teen years people got *nit picky* about long hair or short hair for boys, today probably ear rings. In the larger scheme of things, we should care less about the *outer* things and more on moral issues where we should be like a rock, because they will do great damage. God's laws are a love gift to us; when we break them, we break ourselves.

One day, case in point, when the known church gossip, let's call her Mazie, was at our home, Kathleen came down the stairs dressed in a short black skirt, black leotards, black jersey , black leotards wrapped around her head like a turban and black lipstick and heavy black eye makeup. (No, of course, she wasn't a challenging child). Oh, the repercussion from our Mazie, the known gossip in the room. "I've never seen such an ugly outfit in my entire life." She had had quite a long life. "You're surely not going out in that, are you?" Kathleen sat down on my lap.

I nervously laughed and said, "Kathleen, dear. What are you doing?" (She looked like a dilapidated drug addict or something worse.) Now, clothes are an amoral issue, even though it gets harder and harder to sort that out with the fashions of today. Was I to follow my principles or save my pride in front of that woman?

Hang on; the situation became worse when the door bell rang. Kathleen leaped up and let in a handsome young man dressed in a long black coat, black pants and shoes. Spiked hair! Mazie had already judged the situation and we were all found guilty. As it turned out the kids were going to the mall on a lark just to see what peoples' reactions would be, not the beginning of a downward spiral of depravity. I let her go. If I were going to crack down on our daughter, it would be over a moral issue. That is always hard to do, especially in front of our Mazie. As it turned out, the mall visit was innocent, not the beginning of a rebellious heart. *Thank you Lord!* Actually, aside from the black lipstick that I thought looked ghastly, Kathleen looked kind of cute, the dark leotards covered what the skirt didn't. *Excuses, excuses.*

In high school, parents must create good and appropriate disciplines. Each child responds differently, forcing trial and error strategies for us in order to be effective in child rearing.

One of my children had a very strong will (OK, it was our daughter, the second child. Are you catching on?) What disciplining technique worked on her had no effect on or appropriateness for Tim.

One exhausting day, after grounding Kathleen for almost eleven weekends in a row for talking disrespectfully to me, I insightfully concluded, (I'm quick), grounding her was not even a little bit effective. I prayed, "Lord what should I do? What I'm doing with my daughter is not working." One of those genius answers from God came floating into my mind.

"Kathleen, I want you to meet with me for one hour each day for the next month. I will direct the program; you will do whatever I desire. I have ten books for you to read and we will discuss them after you read them (She loved to read). I picked out books like: *In His Steps, Shadow of the Almighty, How to Win Friends and Influence People.*

My prescription may not be easy for working moms, but you can find the time or create your own *what works*. Kathleen met with me everyday and read the books. Also in that hour I taught her things like baking pies, cakes and preparing dinners, how to set a table and a little bit about how to sew. We did some discipleship lessons and discussed the books. Years later I discovered she told her boss that those were the best punishments or disciplines I had ever given her. *A wee blessin' ta ye, me child.* Now she uses the same technique with her children. *Saints preserve us.*

Kathleen is now the Resident Director of a 500 student dormitory at Wheaton college. She intuitively knows every devilish thing the students are going to do before they do it, because she did them all. "He restores the years that the locust have eaten."

Another principle: We purposefully sent our children to the local neighborhood public schools. There they could begin facing different life situations and we could help them deal with the difficulties as they impacted their lives. But in their college years they would be forming their adult philosophies and possibly meeting their mates. We chose for them to attend a Christian college. We told them that we would pay for any Christian college they chose to go to. *Choice within limits.* They both chose Wheaton College. Of course, a Christian college is no guarantee of a Pollyanna, no stress, no trouble college experience, but it sure gives the opportunity for young people to develop a biblical life view from godly professors and by being around intelligent, Christian students from around the world.

Currently there is a debate going on in the Christian world about the necessity for specifically Christian elementary schools and home schooling. In my wizened years, I have seen students in Christian schools turn out great and badly and students who have gone to a secular school turn out just fine and badly. To say the obvious, each child is unique. We thus need to pray about what is best for each individual child. Take heart, there is no perfect, always right answer for every child. And right now two of our grand children are being home schooled.

"Before *I got married I had six theories about bringing up children, now I have six children and no theories.*" Lord Rochester 1675

A young expert on child behavior frequently delivered a lecture called "Ten Commandments for Parents". He married and became a father. The title of the lecture was altered to "Ten Hints for Parents". Another child arrived; the lecture became uggestions for Struggling Parents." A third child was born and he stopped lecturing.

Chapter 14
WORMWOOD IS CLEVER

From the time our children could close their little hands around a penny, we began to teach them about tithing. They would clutch their little, sweaty penny on their way to Sunday school, or when they sat in church, I (Roger was preaching) would always give them a coin. When the offering plate passed down our row they would eagerly watch its approach, and then cheerily put the coin in the velvet-bottomed plate. At home we would talk about how their money would help feed the poor and hurting people around the world and along the way teach people about God. (I wish my pennies went that far.)

When our son Tim reached the ripe age of nine he was watching a telethon on Christian TV that showed the needy and hungry children in Africa and the rest of the world. He was very moved by the plight of so many children and decided he wanted to give his *whole* weekly allowance (now up to 25 cents) to the needy—for the rest of the year. We said, "Tim, you realize that you will have no spending money if you do that. How about giving 50%? Tim insisted on 100%. "Well, OK then."

Faithfully Tim remembered to give all of his allowance each week.

Strange about family traditions: when I was Tim's age my mother would always say, "You can never out-give God."

(In my experience that has always been true.) My Scottish born mother would also say, "Shovel out your money to God, and God shovels money back to you. God's shovel is bigger than your shovel." I, of course, repeated those mantras, believed them and experienced their truths.

That year proved the point to Tim. What he gave that year probably added up to not much more than five dollars; but what he experienced was extremely unusual that year. He won: two new $100 bikes *and* a free trip to Wheaton College's Honey Rock Camp in Wisconsin.

But it didn't take long for the crafty, enticing Wormwood of C.S. Lewis' *Screwtape Letters* to stop by Tim's young, fertile, imagination.

Tim began thinking, "Hey, this is a good deal. I mean, really. I figure that I'll just give my entire tithe again next year to see what I can get." Somewhere in Tim's early spiritual journey his motives had became just a little tainted.

Recognize the symptoms? I do.

Chapter 15
HOLIDAYS

Halloween? Not so big. A few tiny Tootsie Rolls and some candy corn and a silly home made costume. St. Patrick's Day? Nothing. Hardly even a shamrock or anything green appeared. But our kids, Tim and Kathleen, always looked forward to each of *our* traditional holidays.

Roger and I, well mostly I, loved all the glitz, the tinsel, the jingle bells, and huge Christmas trees, with the idea that they were symbols—mostly pagan carry-overs from another era—wonderful, colorful reminders of one of the two most important days in history. We were always happy when the southern towns we lived in decorated all the streets for the Christmas Holidays. God did come to earth, and the galaxy of lights, and wreaths and trimmings were constant reminders to us that something important had happened, and we were celebrating. The day after Thanksgiving the Christmas dishes came out and were used daily for our meals; the drinking glasses were changed to red and green. The kids loved it and so did I.

In writing about Christmas years later, I laugh—and feel terribly nostalgic about our family times together. Part of the laughing memory was how we could put a little pressure on the kids to be good by singing, "You better watch out, you better not cry, you better not pout I'm telling you why. Santa Claus is coming to town.

Our Advent Wreath always went in the middle of the kitchen table (I'm not sure why, but it had to be there). We had the traditional, symbolic five candles to be lit one at a time every Sunday afternoon, while the larger, white Christ candle was lit on Christmas morning. We lit the candle for the week and read the appropriate scripture and sang a Christmas carol. Kathleen wanted the candles to shine brighter so we began the ritual of pulling down all the window shades in the room when we lit the candles. The candles really glowed. Of course, we explained over and over why we gave gifts at Christmas—because God *gave us* the greatest gift on that day.

Leading up to Thanksgiving and Christmas we would make cookies together, buy a turkey, sweet potatoes, fruits, vegetables, can goods etc., and our children would go with us to deliver the love to a truly needy family appointed by the Salvation Army. Our intent, and hooray for that, was our beginning to teach Jesus' principle: *as you have done it to the least of these, my brethren, you have done it unto me.* We threw in some firm reminders to the kids about how we should act when we delivered to the poor the beautifully packaged bounty. It takes time to discover that even though we have the admonition to *do unto the least of these,* there is the rocky place of feeling very good indeed, and missing how the disadvantaged must feel about being on the receiving end. It is *more blessed* to give, but we shared with our children that it can be tough to receive and we must be careful about our attitude toward those we tried to help. And who was that terrible man who muttered: I thank God that I am not as other men?

THANKSGIVING

Being busy with church activities during Thanksgiving, our young family didn't have enough time very often to get to our extended family's homes. So we would invite friends or older neighbors who didn't have a place to celebrate that year. We often looked up an exchange student or two from the local university and brought them in as family. We were not going to celebrate Thanksgiving alone.

And anyway, I loved decorating for the holiday: fruit, vegetables, flowers. At each plate I would place a card with a decoration and a Bible verse on it about giving thanks. I'm sure, looking back, that it was a bit much, but I loved it. And if it's your thing—go for it.

After we all crowded around the festive table, each person would read the little verse I had put on their place card and then we'd give thanks for so many of God's good gifts to us. Of course, I was a little exhausted from getting up at three to start the oven. But I was always buoyed by the crowd and their laughter and chatter.

At the end of the meal Roger would ask everyone in turn, "What were you most thankful for this year?" The stories were always fun to hear—there was always a comedian in the crowd—and encouraging. But above all, our children were learning to be thankful, to behave at the table with adults, and to make their own age appropriate contribution.

CHRISTMAS

Christmas Morning we would always have a special breakfast, frequently homemade goodies that came in the door from our caring church members. We would always read the Christmas story from Luke, light the last Advent candle, the Christ candle, before opening our Christmas gifts one at a time, oohing and awing as we went on for hours. The ritual continues to this day. In their 30's and 40's, when they can make it back to mom and dad's for Christmas, they make sure we do it all correctly. "No, Mom, that's not the way we've always done it. Here, let me.)

Traditions are great for building values, memories, important truths that we share and for building a close family.

Never skimp on those times. They are essential, personal, memorable building blocks for each of us. And do not, repeat, do *not* allow your family gatherings to become wearying rehashes of old resentments.

EASTER

On Easter, in our tradition, we always went to a sunrise service at some dreadful, early hour. Of course, that's what one does when you are a part of a clergy family. Once we dragged our bodies out of bed and had a cup of coffee, the sunrise service was always the highlight of the day.

Our church's tradition back then was a program held in a park or in someone's home overlooking the valley below. It was great standing at the edge of the brow with the valley below grey with mist. Everyone bundled in winter coats and sweaters would sing "Up from the Grave He Arose" just as the incredibly stunning sun inched into view, causing red/yellow streaks to shoot from the horizon, bringing a true sense of awe. "He is risen. He is risen, indeed." What a way to visibly bring the reality of Christ's resurrection to our children.

On the secular side of Easter after Sunday school and church, we went to the Country Club. (Well, somebody has to do it.) We had lunch and afterwards the club sponsored an Easter egg hunt for the children.

The first year my feisty kids participated in the hunt, ("They were the preacher's kids. You know what they're like, my dear"), the prize for the most eggs collected was two; count them, two baby ducks. Intuitively I knew our kids would win, not that they were competitive or anything. They took off like Olympians when the whistle blew, scampering up the hill looking in every crevice. They were from a family of road runners.

Of course, there were the sweet little children dressed for the event by Neiman-Marcus, strolling along like *The Sound of Music* von Trapp family, picking up a brightly colored egg here and there and gently putting it in their basket as they smiled warmly back at mommy. Our children—the preacher's kids—were long gone, looking for the eggs as though they hadn't eaten in a week. The whistle blew to stop the hunt, Tim and Kathy came out from the boulders and trees with baskets mounded above the rim, looking a bit tattered. They, of course, won!

Now we had two ducks—baby yellow, cutesy-wootsy little duckies. I reluctantly took them home. Since ducks lived in the water, and I was an indulgent mother, the bathtub became the little yellow fluffs' home. Just in case you should be wild enough or even entertain the notion of getting ducks (duckies) for your young children, don't put them in the tub to live. Ducks swim, ducks eat, ducks poop. (I think I remember that from a biology class.) What a mess!

The next day, Tim and Kathleen decided, before we the aging parents got out of bed, that they would take the ducks down to the creek behind our home to see how they swam. Well, baby ducks know how to swim—but not especially in freezing cold water. There were tentative attempts by the chicks to navigate the artic waters but then the intrepid chicks' heads drooped to their sides as they made a non-cute chick screech. "The ducks' necks are broken! Mommy, Mommy," my little exploring naturalists shrieked as they raced back up to the house.

How does one get near frozen ducks warm was one of my weightier, scientific questions of the day? Madam Currie to the rescue! I dialed the oven to its lowest temperature and put the chicks in a box on the open oven door. The kids were crying that the ducks were going to cook. "They're going to die!" But in five minutes the little duckie's heads popped up, they fluffed their downy, infant feathers and were ready to explore some more. The kids thought I was a miracle worker, and here I thought I was only poor old Eve Currie.

The little ducks walked around our yard with our hope-less dog following them. Tim, our budding animal trainer, thought it was so wonderful that our dog liked the ducks and wanted to play with them. I noticed, rather, a carnivorous gleam in the dog's eyes.

This can only be said in a "Once upon a time..." spooky voice. "One day the ducks were gone!" The children cried and cried, while at the same time swearing that their dog hadn't eaten them.

I didn't try to destroy their fantasy. Good doggie.

Chapter 16
HOW TO FIND TIME WITH YOUR HUSBAND AND CHILDREN

Ah yes, the question that surpasses all questions. How does a busy pastor have quality time with his wife and family? My husband and any conscientious pastor/husband is going to struggle with the issue even if they are aware of the problem. Church work is wonderful but ENDLESS. There is always more your husband could be doing to feel like he is pastoring well. There is always someone else who could have been visited more, hospitals to visit, wedding rehearsals and weddings to attend, and thousands of committee meeting and elders' meetings, funerals, preparations for Wednesday nights and Sunday morning sermons, and Sunday school classes to be taught, counseling appointments and six week premarital counseling sessions, new member classes, breakfast meeting and more and still someone will say…"You didn't visit my Aunt Betty or "What in the world do those ministers do anyway; they only have a sermon to prepare."

Where in all those commitments can you squeak out time for family and children? Good question! A question we struggled with all the time. We both wanted to keep our marriage in good shape and nurture our children well, which takes time. It was always our concern that we might minister to all the people in the church well and yet neglect our children and as a result have them not following the Lord.

When our children were little Roger took Saturday off. Since that was the day our children were home and he could spend time with them and me. Saturday was a difficult day because if he was preaching that week, the sermon was weighing on his mind and the family time had to end at 7:00p.m., so he could review the sermon and get mentally and prayerfully ready. Often times we had a youth coffee house Saturday nights. Monday and Tuesday were better days, but then the children were not at home because of school. The struggles for Roger were always: this is my day off, but I have to mow the lawn and do those things around the house that needed to be done, plus I would like to play tennis some. All this was true and good, but that didn't leave much time for children or me, or even time to do fun things with our friends. And where in his busy schedule did he get his day of rest, which is Sunday for most people. Sunday is one of the busiest days for a pastor. And there lies the dilemma. Here are some of the ways we tried to meet the needs mentioned above.

1. Roger would take each child on a separate day to breakfast most weeks. He allowed them to choose the place and order anything they wanted. Then during breakfast he would ask them questions about what was going on in their life. This gave them individual attention and focus. They loved that time and still talk about it in their adult lives. Meanwhile I had alone time with our other child at home and made some kind of special breakfast and asked all the questions about their life..

2.   We decided, if possible, when there was not a wedding, funeral or some other event, to take a half a day in the morning on Friday for Roger to do the lawn and play tennis, and then Saturday, we could sleep in while the kids made tents with blankets and a card table and emptied our kitchen of pots and pans to make their tent a home. The kids would usually make us pancakes for breakfast and bring them in to us as a weekly surprise. It really was fun, but when we walked into the kitchen, it looked like a cyclone had hit. They used all kinds of pans and bowls and utensils making the pancakes, but they were so pleased to be able to "help". After the pancake delivery, they would lie under the tent and watch an hour of Saturday morning cartoons. After the morning routine we could spend the rest of the day playing with them and going places, or whatever creative thing we came up with. After we put the kids down at night, often we would get a baby sitter and set up the coffee house for the youth group or Roger would have to finish his preparation for the sermon.

3.   Since most of Roger's meetings were at night he would come home at 5:00 or 5:30 and play ball with the children or make something with them, while I was cooking dinner. We would have an early dinner from 5:30 or 6:00p.m. We put our kids to bed early about 7:30 after baths and all. Then we could often tuck them in and then Roger would head out to his meetings. Of course the children were up bright eyed and bushy tailed at 6:00 in the morning.

4.   We made it policy to always eat meals together (breakfast and dinner). It wasn't until they were teenagers that our children realized that most of their friends didn't do anything like that. Those were very special times and so much more meaningful than everyone eating separately.

5.   Vacations were other quality times and memorable moments as a family. Make sure you take your four weeks or what ever time the church gives you. God can take care of His church when you're gone. Since in those early years we were not making much money, our activities were either tent camping with the breakfast aroma of bacon cooking and coffee brewing or visiting family. We fall down and call my brother, Paul and sister-in-law Sally, blessed because they allowed us to come to their big home sometimes for our whole vacation.

Chapter 17

WE ARE SMALL; HE IS NOT

In our fourth church, during our new members' class, one of the young couples came to faith in Christ. The wife, Jeanine, was a very vivacious, enthusiastic and attractive person and happily excited about her new experience with Christ. I asked her if she would like to be a part of a ten week Bible study (always make it time limited) to discover how she could learn to put her new faith into action. She said, "I'd love to!"

"OK, here are four, up front, commitments," I said with a smile.

First, I will be at the Bible Study, unless I am dead, dying, or out of town. Second, I will do a half hour of homework each week. Third, I will learn a memory verse each week. Then I said, "The hardest of all is number four. I will pray that God will give me someone to teach what I have learned." (I made the commitments very clear, so that she knew what she was getting herself into.) I assured her that someday, sometime, God would bring someone across her path that she could teach what she had learned. I really didn't want her to be teaching for a while, since she had zero background in Christian things. But God had different ideas.

We were into our third week of study with four other girls, (We were having great, always laughing, sometimes crying times together.), when I had to go with Roger on a mission trip. While I was gone, out of the clear blue, a non-Christian friend came up to her, and asked, "Will you do a Bible study with me?" Jeanine looked amazed, and said, "Joy said this would happen."

In her panicked heart she thought, "What am I going to do?" But that week she, with her infant knowledge, a study guide and a huge trust in God, led the Bible study with that person and two other non-Christian young women she had invited to come with her. Eventually all three came to faith in Christ.

OK are you ready? Years later one of those three became our church's Christian Education Director; and another became one of our church's most effective care-givers. I have always been a slow learner about God's timing and his ability to create miracles...in spite of a stuttering Moses, too young Jeremiah or a surprised Joy.

"If you think you are too small to make a difference, try sleeping in a closed room with a mosquito." African Proverb

Chapter 18
WHO WOULD HAVE THOUGHT...?

Applying the Bible verse "Not by might, nor by power but by my Spirit says the Lord," is not easily done. For me there had to be lessons again and again with perplexing variety in order for me to begin to put it into practice.

A case in point: in our first church we made friends with a couple we enjoyed a lot. The wife, Kathy, a Christian, was about my age and her husband, Sam, was about twenty years older; he was a non-Christian and an intuitive, practicing psychiatrist. He and Kathy were asked to meet weekly with a group of local pastors and their wives to train us in how to become more sensitive and about counseling techniques for our congregations. We prayed for Sam to come to faith, but he continued to be a charming, humorous, brilliant and a militant agnostic.

In the 60's an evangelical group called *Faith at Work* was very effective at reaching the disinterested and disaffected. So we invited Sam and his wife to go to a *Faith at Work* conference. We were surprised but delighted that Sam decided to go with us. One of the big parts of *Faith at Work* was their small group format. After registration we were all placed in small groups of men and women—all except Sam. He was surprisingly and curiously placed in a group of women: two women clergy, two Mennonite women with their bonnets, and another very shy lady.

When Sam's wife and I heard about the make up of the group we panicked. Sam, the self-styled curmudgeon, would destroy those innocent ladies and he would be so turned off by them.

"Lord, what are you doing?" I thought.

Kathy and I tried everything to get Sam into another group. Forget it. At dinner Sam reported that he had done one of his expert, instant diagnoses, telling the women what was psychologically messed up with each of them. He was proudly and perversely delighted that he even swore at the most frightened woman—so much for our attempts at trying to impact Sam for Christ. Could it be that God was sabotaging our efforts? Nah.

The conference was to conclude on Sunday afternoon, but Kathy reported that Sam decided to go home Saturday evening. "The best laid plans of mice and"...oh, forget it. We were bewildered, for *we* had worked everything out perfectly.

Kathy was totally discouraged and she drove home in stony silence. After a few miles Sam said to Kathy, "When we get home tonight, let's call our friends and invite them to start one of those small groups. They sound interesting. We'll study the Bible, I'll lead it."

Kathy nearly drove the car off the road. Sam went on to say, "Ya know, I threw everything I had at those five, unliberated women. I was going to show them how dumb they were, how up tight they were; they just smilingly loved me back. And, actually, they were bright, too. It slowly dawned on me that they had something going on in their lives that I didn't have." Hmm.

That night Sam called, with unusual enthusiasm for him, a half a dozen of his non-Christian buddies. He told them he was starting a new something or other called a small group. When a good friend you know who thinks little about the Bible calls you and says, "Come on over for a Bible study," you do. Agnostic Sam, a stumbling, dazzling Christian-newborn started his first Bible study that night!

A humorous footnote to this story came about when Sam's boss, the director of the mental hospital, heard Sam had started not a new group, but *a nude group.* The director telephoned Sam to instruct: "I know how good interactive groups can be and how you like them, but probably a nude group is a little over the top. I don't recommend it." That gives you a clue about Sam's reputation.

The conclusion of this episode: all the husbands and wives Sam invited to his home for the new Bible Study Group eventually became Christians.

Why do I write this story? There will be times in your life when you will wonder: "What in the world is the Lord doing? What's going on here?" I've found, in retrospect, that His timing and ways are delightfully and deliciously *right on.* What seems absurd to us is always a part of His perfect plan.

"Work on the mission field is like a man going about with a lit match seeking to ignite anything ignitable. This is what God wants; patches of fire burning all over the world."

China—Jim Frazer 1886-1938

Chapter 19
I FEEL DULL

Each church has a uniqueness of personality—joys, struggles, surprises and lessons to learn.

In our second church, God gave us the experience of an incredible, dynamic, overwhelming spiritual renewal. It swept through our congregation and by extension, even the city. The Spirit of God was like a tiger unleashed for our awesome, sometimes overwhelming adventure. It was a time when God powerfully transformed lives and our congregation. He easily transcended what the pastors, not wanting to get in the way of that glorious outpouring, were doing.

Uniquely there were people of wealth and influence who were touched. As they turned to Christ, they felt the thrall of God and His Spirit and began to use their resources—mind, money and influence—to impact the city and world. They gave generously to inner city ministries. They put the "C" back in the local YMCA. They used their money to impact world missions, to fight pornography and the local abortion clinic. They developed programs to rebuild families and start small group ministries. What an exciting time!

I was thrilled.

But I began to feel dully grey in the midst of the excitement of our people's new births in Christ. One morning I knelt down at my bedroom window. I had frequently looked out on our stunning, surrounding, back yard, where I had often taken walks in the greenery of God's creation. Those memorable times always triggered within me a special praise to the Lord, but not this morning.

During that time of our congregation's jubilations, I had to confess how dull I felt in comparison to those joyously, alive new Christians. Outside my window was a redolent, beautifully fragrant pink rosebush. I said to the Lord, "Those new in their faith are like my roses, but strangely I feel like that old, green maple tree, no fragrance, a dark boring color, not that exciting pink bush. Through tears I said, "Help me be more like those new Christians—beautiful *and* fragrant.

In a split second, without further contemplation, a thought came from God, it was an intuitive gift. *The old maple tree gives shade—it houses nests, produces early leaves and doesn't easily get knocked down when there are storms. Its roots are deep.* When was the last time you had a thought like that?

There I was, the older Christian, a steady, mature person, a shelter for the new Christians. They needed to be fed and helped to grow. I suddenly rejoiced in the place God had put me and reaffirmed that my job was to feed and nurture new Christians. Sure, the storms would come for them, but I could be a shelter and a strong place for them. So I got over my pity party. Thank you, Lord.

That also just happened to be the beginning of a whole new ministry of discipling groups of young women. But the real excitement was the dawning realization that we are all to be sturdy trees that meditate on God's Word—day and night. Then we will bear fruit and our leaves won't wither. We will prosper.

Thus, our job, according to the first Psalm, is to be refreshed from God's majestic and nourishing Word. God's job, in turn, as he generously promised, is to produce fruit in His season.

We *will be* blessed.

If that isn't exciting, then what is?

"Blessed is the man...whose delight is in the law of the Lord and on his law he meditates day and night. He is like a tree planted by streams of water, which yields its fruit in season and whose leaf does not wither. What ever he does prospers. "   Psalm 1: 1-3

Chapter 20
I CAN'T DO IT!

One of those difficult, memorable situations for me came during the eleventh year of Roger's ministry. I was asked by another church's woman's group to speak to their *Women of the Church* retreat to be held at a beautiful place in the woods. Of course, if you are a minister's wife many people have the idea that you automatically have the gift of public speaking, at least as good as Billy Graham.

I was not Billy Graham nor was I even close to being Ruth Graham. I politely declined, but the gracious woman who called was desperately in need of a speaker. She persisted.

"Well," I reluctantly and carefully said, "I'll be happy to organize the retreat for you and find a good speaker."

"But we really want *you* to come and be *our speaker.*" I hated speaking and I was not going to be budged.

I said, even more reluctantly, "I'll pray about it," hoping to find a way out. Sure, I mumbled a token prayer so that if she called again, at least I would be honest about having prayed.

A week later this *very nice*, persistent woman called again. I knew I should have gone to the grocery store that morning. "Well, Joy, do you think you can accept our invitation to speak?"

"Really, I'm not a good speaker as I told you, so I've prepared a list people I'd recommend." She was not to be thwarted. I finally was beginning to think that, maybe I *was* supposed to speak. Could it be that I just need to trust God?

"Oh, all right," I found my self saying without even thinking. Then the anxiety hit my stomach and I felt ill. Even so, my organizing mode kicked in and I said I would bring some women with me so they could share what God has been doing in *their* lives.

"That'll be just so nice, honey."

At least if I failed, those other women would inspire them. I literally prepared for six months and still didn't feel good or even prepared for any of my talks. My anxiety was now reaching incapacitating levels. Should I call our doctor? Why did I say yes? Why did I say *yes!*

After I pulled myself together I invited five women to participate who had recently come alive in their walk with Christ. Then I invited all the women's husbands to meet with Roger the nights we were at the retreat. They were to pray for us. That gave me a slight flicker of hope. At last I was in my comfortable organizing mode.

I planned the whole weekend around the other women sharing before each talk, followed by small groups. I would only speak...briefly. I was beginning to feel better about the whole thing.

The first evening of the conference when I stood to speak I was in a state of panic that had me shaking. I began talking but could not focus on my notes. What I was saying, it seemed to me, sounded pathetic and I wandered off the topic. Sweat trickled down my spine. None of my notes made sense. I paused, took a deep breath then another, and said quietly, "I'm lost." I giggled because I was mortified. I started adlibbing and finally, mercifully I ended. I was so embarrassed, I wanted to hide. My friends looked at me with such kind sympathy. The bad part was the looming dread over the fact that the next morning I was to speak *again*. "Oh, Lord, please" I demanded, "I still don't have this talk straight in my head. Help me! *Please*, or just let me have a medical (nervous breakdown?) emergency that requires me to go to the hospital right now or something!

The next morning my friends and I sat on a log out in the woods. I sobbed and laughed and cried some more. I was pathetic, but I still didn't know what I was going to say. One of my friends said, "Joy, just share that verse you shared with me this morning."

I answered, somewhat abruptly, still wanting to hold onto my pitiful self, "That has *nothing* to do with my talk!"

"Share it anyway." I cried; I was even more pathetic. I'm supposed to be the leader of women? Ha! They prayed. I was sure that of all the women who had come to the retreat for spiritual renewal I was the one most in need. I was having a spectacular, first class pity party. I walked to my death sentence as I slouched up the hill to the auditorium. Furthermore, I wondered, if the men *had* prayed last night and I was such a failure then, what was today going to be like with no men praying? I had enough composure to wipe my tears and freshen my lipstick. There was no turning back. After group singing and a solo, I stood. *Why in the world did I ever say yes to speak at this retreat?*

I cleared my throat and stood there. Why didn't the world end? My eyes swept across the auditorium and then I shared the verse my friend told me to, plus some thoughts about it. I am embarrassed to tell you that the verse was: "Perfect love casts out fear. Tears came to my eyes as the verse ministered to *me*. At that instant my whole talk, from beginning to end, came clear to my mind. The Spirit of God was doing something unusual. I did not look at my notes as I spoke with freedom and power and without fear. As I was speaking, I thought, *Lord I know it's you, don't stop.*

I had never experienced anything like that before. It was as though I had been an instrument that was being played by someone else. A tuba? No, *a harp!* How about God?

At the end of my talk, I noticed women quietly weeping. What should I do; give some kind of invitation? *I hated giving invitations.* But, I did it anyway. Many came forward to rededicate their lives—unusual for Presbyterian women—unusual for me. We prayed. After the prayer, all five of my friends came up and threw their arms around me acknowledging that God had done something great. He had used frightened, untrusting me to accomplish what he wished.

My next talk that weekend was probably as bad as the first one. I was equally certain that God had accomplished what he willed and I had relearned a great lesson. Do you remember Moses when he said, "Lord I can't go to Pharaoh; I stutter." Moses felt as weak and inadequate as I did...the difference being that he had a burning bush with him.

But God kept saying, "Moses, who made your mouth? I, God, can accomplish anything I want through any inadequate, bumbling instrument I want, any time I choose."

At the conference my goal was to be a great speaker, but God rather wanted to show forth *His* greatness. A great lesson from God. A lesson I need to be reminded of many times.

Jesus said to his disciples as he was sending them out: "At that time you will be given what to say, for it will not be you speaking, but the Spirit of your Father speaking through you" Matthew 10: 19-20

Another Such Moment

I seemed to be cursed by having to swim in water too deep for me. For example, I was asked (coerced?) to be on the committee (that's easy) for the "Congress of Renewal" for the whole Presbyterian denomination. I also was asked to be in charge of prayer at this huge convention which was to be held in Dallas, Texas, everything's huge in Texas.

At the final planning committee for the congress the chairman announced that each of the people on committees was going to lead a workshop. Many very famous people would be speaking: Leighton Ford, Lloyd Olgilvie (then chaplain of the US Senate), Bill Bright, leader of *Campus Crusade* and many other Christian luminaries. My initial panic thought was, *oh, no, not again.* Speaking? But I had learned. This time I said, "OK, Lord, here we go again. You're in charge."

I decided I'd do a workshop on discipling Women. When I arrived at the event, they told me I would know how many were going to be in my group by the size of the room assigned. I was an unknown, so I felt certain I would be in one of the remote clothes closets.

After wandering around the conference center I finally found my conference room. It was the size of a college gymnasium. "Oh my, there must be a mistake." When the time came for the seminar, I walked into the room just before Vonette Bright; wife of *Campus Crusade's* President, entered to hear me talk. She had written many books on discipleship. I greeted her warmly but was chuckling inside: OK, Lord, is this a test? The second thought was, "Well, Father, you have put me here in this position again and unless you enable me, as you enabled Moses, nothing good will happen here other than a bigger blunder." This time one of those holy boldness moments came over me and I enjoyed the process. Old dogs *can* learn new tricks. I was comfortable and trusting.

Chapter 21
DOES MY LIFE COUNT?

Roger and I, as I have said, frequently worked together when he was an associate pastor. He would do all the up front talking, teaching things, and I would do the detail work: the planning and programming, phone calling, helping with games, sitting in on the Bible studies, talking with individuals, counseling. I loved it all, but having majored in Christian Education, I began to feel that I just wasn't spiritually impacting anyone directly.

One morning at the breakfast table, I shared my feelings with Roger. I was a little teary, as intimacy is not easy for me (even with my husband) or just maybe it was **that** time of the month. Roger rather wisely and gently asked if I were willing to do *anything* God wanted me to do. Yes, don't be silly; of course.

He said, "Let me just pray that if you are to be doing something different, God will show you. (Don't pray that prayer unless you mean it!) After praying I felt better. Roger had helped to put things into perspective. Interestingly enough, a week earlier I had received from one of my former Young Life girls a list of questions that she used discipling women on Capital Hill in Washington. She was an assistant to Senator Mark Hatfield. I put those three pages on my refrigerator with a magnet in case, someday, I might need it.

That day I received a call from one of our college students who had been in our youth group. He said, "My sister-in-law, a pharmacist, wants to know if you would disciple her." I thought, oh my, I have never had any one *ask me* to do this before, (I was always the asker). I didn't even know the sister-in-law. My thought was: Hmm, God, you work fast. He was responding to the prayer Roger had prayed that morning. I called a friend, Mary Pat, another young mom, and said, "You'll never guess what happened to me today." I recounted the story, and she laughed and rejoiced with me. The next day, she called me back, "Joy, I just asked five girls if they wanted to join us in a Bible study with you. I hope you don't mind. Would you be willing to teach us what you are teaching the pharmacy girl?"

You'd better duck when you pray prayers like I did.

That Sunday we invited the new members' class to our house for dinner. One young woman asked, "Would you disciple me?" *What was going on here?* No one had ever asked me to do that before and now I had seven people in one week asking me to disciple them. Clearly God was at work in answer to Roger's and my simple prayer.

I took the discipleship sheets off the refrigerator and the next week I had three, count them, three groups to pour my life into. I had every person in each group make four commitments: be at the meetings, do the homework, pray for the group members and pass on to someone else what you learn. I didn't think the pharmacist, who had little spiritual background, would ever teach anyone else what we were learning. However, two years later I received a phone call from her asking me if I had any more of those discipleship questions' list. You bet I did. She told me she worked with another pharmacist who wanted her to disciple her. Yes, yes! God is faithful.

When I was a student at Wheaton College, Major Ian Thomas, a renowned speaker from England, said *"It's not your ability, but your availability that God wants."*

That has been proven to me over and over again.

Chapter 22
JOYS OF MINISTRY

I hadn't realized when I became the wife of a minister what joy there would be in being on the inside of church life. Within the church family so much of life's highs and lows go on daily and often few people hear about them. But since I was my husband's confidante I became a part of so many people's life-changing experiences. So often they increased my faith: relationships that were falling apart were renewed, people without faith came to faith in Christ, and others were called into ministry to serve Christ. It was always very meaningful to be the pastor's wife for weddings, funeral, church functions, worship services, parties for the staff, and those many church dinners (churches love dinners), and church retreats in some far off mountain hideaway. Many wives, sadly never become a part of their husband's activities. It's easy to slip into living separate lives.

THE BEST PART
CHANGED LIVES

In one of our churches Roger and I wanted to start a small group Bible study. After the first study, Roger said to the group sitting comfortably in a friend's home, "You guys are great! This is what a small group is supposed to be like. What would you think about continuing the group for an eight week series?"

A young wife and mother, we'll call her Carrie, said with a bored tone, "To tell the truth, I'm really not interested in a Bible study," Without prompting she continued to tell us why she felt the way she did. "When I was about twelve I went to a Billy Graham Crusade. I went forward at Graham's invitation and consequently was eager to follow Christ. Nothing was really going on in my church and no one helped me discover what should be my next steps for my new faith. I tried very hard to be a good person. But I soon gave up. I just wasn't interested any more. As a matter of fact, I felt abandoned and angry!"

Everyone in the room identified with her disappointed teen years. We explained to her that her experience was like a newborn being left without food, love, changed diapers, or being washed and powdered. Soon the abandoned baby would become very ill, and would look very dead. Like that baby, Carrie had no one to spiritually nurture her and she began to feel dead.

In her usual perky way she said, "OK, then I'll give the group a chance." Her husband wanted in on it too. That study continued for three years, after which the group's members began leading their own groups. Carrie has been a spiritual mentor for many women. Another man became a significant corporate contributor to mission organizations and ministries. What could be greater than God allowing us to be a tiny part of impacting that group and the world for Christ.

Another story: A husband and wife, pretty wild in college, were now well into their thirties, but were still involved with drugs and drinking. Somehow this handsome couple wanted to be a part of our couple's Bible Study. Why? No one was sure...probably just for social reasons and the word was out that we had a good time at these meetings. Being an extravert, the husband, George, participated as though he had been a part of the group for years—probably the president. At the end of each evening we always asked if anyone had a prayer request. Not missing a beat that first night, George wanted us to pray for a woman at his company who was a single parent. "She's a great worker and she needs the income," he said, "but I have to let her go. I don't want to do it, but I have to this week." Our prayer was to be that he would know when to tell her and be able to do it in as kind a way as possible.

The next week he came bounding into the group shouting, "It works! It works! Prayer works!" We all asked what had happened.

He related, with continued delight, that he had gone into work the next day and first thing in the morning the woman came to his office unannounced and said with tears in her eyes, "I love working here very much, and I hate doing this, but I must leave. I have another job that will pay me more. I am so sorry!" George couldn't believe his ears. God had answered his prayer!

Today, George is an elder in his church, living for Christ, leading a small group and always discipling younger men. Because of their enthusiastic and winsome witness, he and his wife are impacting for Christ many young couples' lives. To be a part of people's life-changing moments, brings the best kind of satisfaction in anyone's life.

Chapter 23
A NEED I DIDN'T KNOW I HAD

When we arrived at our "Mountain Mission" church I had three pairs of shoes, black for dress, brown for every day and white for summer. My dresses had missionary-barrel distinctiveness about them, but they matched my shoes. It began to dawn on me that I was a curiosity in the midst of the fashion-wise of our church. Happily or dumb, that didn't bother me. "If you're clean and neat and have *just a little* fashion sense, you'll be OK," my mother always assured me.

However, after about two weeks on "the mountain", I was invited to a luncheon where *the ladies* were going to welcome me to the church. I was at the table with one of the "most fun" women; we laughed and just hit it off. We talked about books we liked and shared in common, funny stories about our families. I felt as though I were accepted.

About a week after the luncheon, I received a phone call from this lady. We were chatting on about nothing significant or gossipy, when she very gingerly and graciously said, "My college daughter usually gets all new clothes each season, and I'm left with her last year's clothes to pack away. I was wondering if you could use them? I'd rather give them to someone I know, than to Goodwill."

I said, "Oh that would be just wonderful!" *I was slowly learning how to be a Southern Lady.* Little did I know what incredible treasures would be coming through the door? Wool jackets, leather jackets, matching skirts, top of the line slacks, fifteen pairs of designer shoes (just the right size) of beautiful quality, leather pocketbooks to match, blouses, sweaters, Christian Dior night gowns and peignoir sets and evening gowns—on and on. I couldn't believe it. What a gift from this woman and what a gift from God to help me be "All things to all men and women that I may win some." I was now dressed better than (for that day) Jacquelyn Kennedy. (Well, almost.) I experienced God's provision over and over again, in the most improbable ways, during our years in ministry. You will too.

Roger is now retired from the pastorate. One Christmas after retirement our children and grandchildren were home for the holidays. Our son, Tim, mentioned he missed all the goodies from the church members we used to receive at Christmas. I chuckled and thought to myself, "Oh yes, what a great memory." There were always wonderful and kind gifts that came in our front door from many of our friends in the church—either special home made goodies or gifts of various sizes and shapes, but always, there was a breakfast pastry made especially for our Christmas morning. They were wonderful moments of love each holiday. What a privilege to be a pastor's wife.

Chapter 24
THE CARING
CHURCH

Being in ministry you must know that you are seldom going to have lots of money. So along the way there will be such major questions as: "How are we going to pay for our children's college?" I quote my mother's response to me when I had such questions, "Joy, where is your faith! Just trust the Lord. He has promised to provide."

Sure, I knew that, of course, God would take care of me and I needn't be anxious about our children's education or the other little necessities of life. But on a $7,000 a year salary those doubts and worries kept creeping in.

A case in point: Our children were in the local public school on the mountain. It was kindergarten through sixth. After sixth grade most of the children went to one of the private schools in town because, (1) there was no junior or senior high school on the mountain, and (2) the public schools were not very well run and had poor academic standards, plus (3) there was great racial strife at that time in our country's history. Needless to say, private schools were beyond our meager clergy budget. But we discovered that someone in our church, not to worry, always paid tuition for pastor's children. What a gift! Consequently, our children received some of the best junior and senior high school educations possible. As for college, we are still not quite sure how we financially got through those years. On paper we didn't make enough money for our kids to go to other than the local state school, nor were we able to save as much as we thought we'd need, but somehow, with our savings, some small academic grants and government loans, we made it through. And both children graduated with only small college loan debts.

Now as a family we laughingly tell and retell the story about Roger trying to save money in our college tuition-broke years. Roger, the financially concerned provider, decided that one of the great saving ways that would make ends meet was to keep our house at 55 degrees, even in our very cold, snowy part of the country. If I wanted to be warm I was to keep the fireplace/wood stove going all day when I was home, I could turn the oven on in the kitchen when preparing meals, and when we took showers, we could turn a heater on in the bathroom. I wore a hat, socks and a sweater to bed. We kept a fire going in the fireplace twenty-four hours a day for six months of the year. I heroically, complainingly, did my part to save money. My husband's tight Dutch heritage showed forth in every frugal lowered degree, but we saved money. I froze, but our children went to college. Roger now apologizes—profusely—for putting the family through those frostbitten years.

One of the funny, ironic footnotes to those penny pinching, heat saving years was that our biggest pay raise came *after* our children graduated from college. No more college bills. "His ways are past finding out."

Chapter 25
GOD'S PROVISION

I am not a health-wealth person who thinks that God wants me and all of you to be rich; but I am aware that God delights in providing when we trust.

Case in point: Roger, because he was officiating, and I were invited to a very formal wedding rehearsal dinner. In those days, ancient history, really, that meant I had to wear a floor length gown. But, I was the poor cleric's wife and thus didn't have one.

I busily did my usual check at the Junior League Bargain Mart and the other places I could find an appropriate dress for the occasion—a *very low* price was the key to my success. The Salvation Army was good—maybe some grand dame of taste had given a beautiful gown to their discount store. No such luck. There was nothing anywhere that could be bought on my budget of $20.00.

I prayed: "Lord, you know I need something appropriate to wear to the wedding party. Help me find something." That afternoon my friend who had a daughter who wore my size called. "Joy, I have a few things I want to bring over for you."

Aha, the wedding reception dress. Yes! I could hardly wait until she arrived and busied myself with picking up the kid's toys. Of course, Sally knew nothing of my need, but, whatever, she had great taste.

Finally she was at the door burdened down with a load of beautiful, hardly worn cloths: suits, jackets all great colors. "How can I thank you. You're so kind." After she left I, as though doing an inventory at Neiman-Marcus, went through the elegant outfits, looking for the gown.

No gown—but there *was* a lovely black suit, I looked great in it and, well maybe, I could wear it to the rehearsal dinner. Sure, I was disappointed, for I thought the timing of Sally's magnificent donations meant an answer to my prayer. Anyway, I finally got my head on straight, in the scheme of things, what difference would it make? A suit, a gown? And did I remember that there were people in our world without any shoes, and I just wanted to show off. (Sounds just like my mother whispering in my head.)

One hour later, Sally called again, "Joy, I'm so sorry, and I hate to bother you, I forgot something I had in the trunk of the car. Can I bring it over, if you're not on the way out, or something?" My heart leaped. I knew it would be a gown. I argued with myself, preparing, just in case, it wasn't a Cinderella Off-to-the-Ball gown.

Sally, when she arrived, opened the trunk, and there was a beautiful designer gown, in just the right color, much nicer than anything I could have ever dreamed of or been able to afford. I told Sally the story and we both wept as I gave her a great hug. I had not previously told her about my need for a gown.

Another moment: I had always been aware that the God of the universe is also a God of loving detail. One night as I was making dinner and standing at the kitchen sink preparing a dinner for some friends, I was thinking through the dinner. I thought, wouldn't it would be nice to have some fresh flower for a centerpiece on the table. Those thoughts were whispered into a prayer, "Lord, it would be so nice to have some flowers." I often tossed up to God prayers about things on my heart and mind.

I hardly had prayed that prayer when one of our college students came walking up the drive with a big handful of daffodils. As much as I know God supplies, I still couldn't believe how the daffodils yellow was just perfect with my color scheme.

Thank you so much, Lord. Thank you.

"We have not because we ask not.." And, Malachi 3:10-12, *"Bring all the tithes and offerings into the storehouse so there will be enough food in my Temple. If you do, I will open the windows of heaven for you. I will pour out a blessing so great you won't have enough room to take it in! Try it! Let me prove it to you! Your crops will be abundant, for I will guard them from insects and disease. Your grapes will not shrivel before they are ripe. Then all the nations will call you blessed, for your land will be such a delight, says the Lord Almighty."*

Chapter 26
WHAT'S MINE IS YOURS

A few years back (don't make me count) we often had our twenty by twenty foot den full of high school and college students. However, I began to discover that soft drinks were being spilled on our new gold rug and our newly covered gold couch. There was one particular college girl, Sarah, who seemed to have less coordination than the others and *always* spilled her grape or orange drink, never a 7-Up. The build up of dark stains made the room a little embarrassing when adults came to our home. The "spiller" also often was our baby sitter at the time. One evening when we came home she laughingly told us that for dinner she had baked chicken for our children, leaving all the innards in the chicken, including the paper! "I didn't know I was supposed to take that stuff out." Betty Crocker she wasn't.

Don't go away, there's more. "Uh, something else, I think I melted your tea kettle. I guess the water must've just boiled away when I was watching TV." The aluminum from the kettle had melted and wrapped itself around the electric coil on the stove.

What was there to say? Trying to fill the awkward silence, I showed Sara a little waste basket Roger had made for Tim's room and how he had painted the desk an antique green. As I was talking, accidentally, clumsily, Miz Sarah took the trash container from my hand and accidentally dropped it on the newly painted desk, chipping it and breaking the corner off the handmade waste basket.

As we stood with our mouths open in utter amazement, we thought: What are we to do? We have a choice to have people in our home whom we want to love and witness to or have a clean, antiseptic, beautiful showplace. We knew what the answer *should* be…but our poor desk and rug…

Not long after, Roger and I went to a seminar that made us a bit uncomfortable. We began to realize more clearly that our furniture had been given to us by God. We were merely stewards of it. God could take care of his property as he wanted to. Our job was to serve His people. People were more important then furniture, rugs or household goods. (Of course, we were to do our best to take care of that which had been given to us, but we're always challenged to make the better choice.)

After the stained rug, marred desk and broken trash basket, we relaxed when unintended mishaps happened. High school students would be high school students. Our house and furniture were God's property and we learned graciously never to say a word.

Roger had often said, "So much food had been spilled on our carpet that if there were ever a famine in our country, all we would need to do was cut our rug into two inch squares, put them in boiling water, and we'd at least have soup for a year." Then one day, we received an envelope from the youth group with money in it to have our rug steam cleaned. Teenagers are great!

Another fun story about furniture and a caring youth group: One Sunday night at youth group time I wasn't feeling very well, so I opted to stay home. About ten minutes later the whole youth group arrived to have their meeting *at our house,* just so I could be a part of it. At the end of the youth group, which went especially well that night—lots of laughter, thoughtfulness and prayer—the leader announced that they had a birthday present for me. *Oh, no!* I like to give gifts but it is hard for me to receive them. I opened a nicely wrapped box. Inside was an awkwardly ugly gift, a grotesque contemporary cross made from three inch flat nails fastened to gold choker. It was nothing I would wear. These pretty sophisticated kids surprised me by their bad taste in jewelry. I couldn't imagine they thought their gift was a beautiful necklace. As I put it on, the top of the nail cross stuck in my chin, while the bottom of the cross began to poke my neck. But I wasn't going to let on how it felt. I loved those kids and said, "Thank you, thank you so much."

One of the girls, whose taste I had always admired, asked, "Do you like it?"

I lied and everyone burst into laughter. They shouted through more gales of laughter, "The real gift is *underneath* the necklace." I lifted the velvet covered cardboard and there was $350. The note with it said, "This money is to have your couch that we've messed up recovered. With much love," and the signatures of all the kids.

That was another example of how our gracious God and those loving kids took care of our aging furniture. I learned a new lesson about God's faithfulness when He and those incredible young people took care of the furniture entrusted to us.

Chapter 27
WHERE ELSE DO YOU FIND SUCH LOVE?

I always enjoyed having exchange students live in our home. It's great to discover other cultures and be apart of a young person's developing years. It was always interesting and, for the most part, fun. Usually Roger and I and the whole church community were a help to the students. We loved sharing our country with each one. We had four students from Germany, three from Argentina and one each from Russia, Uzbekistan, and Mexico. It was our meager opportunity to try and make an impact on young people's lives for God's kingdom.

One such Christian student from Mexico offered a totally different and unexpected experience. She came to the United States to work on her English. Simple enough. She was charming in her own Latin way, wonderful and helpful around the home; pleasant and eager to please, a leader in organizational skills that she used in our church's College and Career Group. Each day she was diligent with her English studies, staying with them way into the night. I was thinking that we could easily have Maria stay a little longer than her planned few months; perhaps she could attend our local university.

I hadn't really been paying that much attention but, I think it was some time after Maria's second month in our home that I began to notice some, well, peculiar moments, signals actually. Maria was becoming very possessive of me, as well as jealous of others. If she went to a movie, she would come home and obsessively talk to me about it, and only with me, asking questions about the movie's seemingly magical and distorted interpretations.

I finally called a friend in Mexico who knew her and asked if she had ever observed her increasingly worrisome behavior? She hadn't. So I just gave Maria's rather strange actions less thought.

Sunday morning a week later, Maria dramatically burst into my bedroom while I was dressing. She was screaming, "Blood is coming out of my mouth! Blood is coming out of my mouth!"

There was no blood that I could see, so in my effort to calm her down I told her in a quiet, *There, there* controlled tone, that there was *no* blood. She became increasingly and frighteningly panicked. She ran screaming throughout the house. Wouldn't you know, Roger had already left to preach at early church.

What should I do? I needn't have gotten an "A" in 101 psychology to know Maria was having a psychotic break and she and I needed help, big time. Now, added to the frantic scenario there were imaginary people and animals outside. She pulled away as I tried to calm her and ran out the door and down the middle of the street. Fortunately it was Sunday so there weren't any cars on our street.

After I got her back in the house, I phoned our church to get help. "It's Joy," I whispered in my best panicked stage voice, "Send someone over right away! I need help." An august elder, dressed in his Sunday best suit, arrived a few minutes later.

At the same time Maria stormed in and made a deep bow before him. Our wise and kind elder looked bewildered.

"I think I need some help here, Mr. Ashley." I hadn't yet been able to tell him of my concerns. Just then Maria leaped onto the couch and jumped up and down. She was terrified at all the scary people outside our windows. There were none.

Mr. Ashley: "I'll call Jack Myers." Jack was a doctor and an elder in our church. In moments, Jack and my friend, Margaret, a counselor from our church showed up. (It was the first time that I was really appreciative of the fact that our home was so close to the church.) Our instant medical team quickly assessed the situation. Another friend came from the church just to pray. (All this care came from one phone call. I was feeling better all the time.)

Add this to the equation; one of the administrators of the local hospital was also a member of our congregation and Margaret quickly called him on his cell phone before the services would begin. "I'd be happy to come over, now don't you get worried." (I love those Southern gentlemen.) Within minutes we practically had the entire medical community in our front living room, all of them knowledgeable and efficient and caring. The hospital they sent us to was a very good one, everybody's first choice, but very expensive. How glad I was to be part of a loving, caring congregation.

Margaret, what a great friend, drove us to the local emergency room. The attending resident gave Maria a strong sedative that he said would calm her for twenty-four hours. Yet in less than an hour Maria, like a young filly, was up and ramming around the emergency room. She was in the manic phase of her illness.

If the psychiatric wing of our local hospital did not have a bed available at the moment, we were told, we would have to take Maria an hour and a half away to the state hospital. Whatever do people do who don't have support systems or money and have a psychotic person in their home?

The next morning the hospital president, Johnny Miller, that glorious, thoughtful member of our church called to tell me that Maria could be admitted to his hospital that morning. "Thank you, Johnny. You have no idea how I appreciate your help. I was truly panicked. May God bless you for all you've done." We hung up and I added, "Thank you too, Lord."

Getting Maria into the car to go to the hospital was, at the very least, difficult. She was so very fearful and became like a colicky baby, legs and arms stiffened, being forced into a high chair. It took three of us to get her in the car. Where were the sedatives and orderlies now that we needed them?

There's more. If you know about signing a person into a psychiatric facility, then you'll understand what happened next. The hurdle was to get Maria to sign herself in. Being over eighteen, she was an adult and she had to sign herself in. When the nurse gave Maria the admitting form to sign, Maria, with a strange grin, held the pen and signed her name in the air. I thought to myself, "What if she doesn't sign? What's plan B? Lord, please help her sign, no, *make* her sign." I think I added, "Now!" I was exhausted.

"Maria," the nurse said quietly in her most therapeutic voice, "these nice people, are your *good* friends. They just want to help you." I was holding my breath. Maria signed.

"O, Lord," I thought to myself, "What would we have done if she *hadn't* signed?" We were told by the admitting physician that with the right medications Maria would probably be out of the hospital in three to five days. "We'll call you, and, of course, you can visit."

Two months later Maria was still in the hospital. The attending physician hadn't discovered the right combination of medicines that were just right for her. When I visited every day I could sense that there *were* positive changes happening. I reported my observations to the psychiatrist. His retort, "Joy, you obviously have friends in high places, because after five days I generally would have sent any patient like Maria to the state hospital." I smiled; of course I had a Friend in high places. As a matter of fact, I had two friends in high places: God and a friend in the regional medical center. After, two months, a new medicine came on the market. It worked! Soon the real Maria was back, not 100%, but close to her old self. With the new medicine, and with a little more time, she would be totally well.

After coming home Maria and I both felt that she needed to go to her home in Mexico, but we both knew that it was too soon for her to travel by herself. Our church elders, when they heard, offered to pay for Maria's aunt to fly to our city and accompany Maria back home. Wow! What a loving church.

Subsequently, we were told that the hospital would absorb all that it cost for Maria to remain hospitalized for two months. An impressive gift.

I really believe Maria came to the states and our home, not for English lesson, but for her to be free enough to express her latent illness and find the medicines that would be effective for her. It turned out that both Maria's mother and brother off and on had severe, mental problems. The medication that finally worked was not even available in Mexico at that time.

Maria's psychiatrist gave her several thousand dollars' worth of free medicine that would last her the two years until it became available in Mexico. How thoughtful and kind he was. How good God was to one of his hurting children and to me.

Maria is now married. She graduated from college and is teaching English!

Her psychotic episode and my first, shaky response to it was one of the hardest experiences in my life. But to experience how the Body of Christ came together made it worthwhile. Now to know that Maria and her family are happy and functioning, beautifully tops all of the charts of those who had prayed and cared.

Chapter 28
BAD DOGGIE

Do you remember that cute little puppy I told you about earlier, the one that was given to us the second week after we moved into our beautifully decorated manse with its manicured, deeply green lawns; the cuddly little puppy, the dervish dancer that the lady who gave the house to the church didn't want, the tail wagging delight of tan fur? Remember?

Now, six months after Coco's arrival, our church was hosting the renowned, Wheaton College Chapel Choir. That Sunday morning the choir was to give its concert, but I had to leave early to teach Sunday school. I told the two choir girls who were bunking in with us, "Don't forget to take Coco outside and tie her up before you leave." They were playing "roll the ball" on the living room floor with the not so little puppy. Coco loved his new playmates.

"Okay," they chirped.

After a great worship service, I chatted with parishioners then strolled home through the newly budded cherry trees. Roger was on the porch, (strange) hands on his hips, looking very angry (uh oh).

"Who left the dog in the house?" He was more than *very angry*. I was not eager to go inside. What I saw was that every curtain, including the ones over the kitchen sink, was pulled down (how the *adorable* Coco managed that I'll never know). Most of them were shredded. The shutters in the bedroom, bathroom and den were demolished. There was a tattered rip in the middle of our antique George Washington bedspread. The wooden window mullions in the den had been chewed down to the glass. I was, at the very least, horrified. What in the world were we going to do now? We didn't have money for new curtains, or bed spreads (it was an antique given to us by Roger's mother), or shutters—let alone new windows. The church women had made our manse so beautiful, as a gift for our moving in, and now what? I called Katherine, the senior pastor's wife, and sobbed as I told her the story.

Katherine said," Don't tell a soul! I'll be right over." When she arrived minutes later, she kept saying as though it were a mystifying mantra, "Oh, no! Oh, no! Oh, no!" Then like a warm and kind friend she said: "Let's see how we can unbend the curtain rods and we'll try to sew together the unripped panels of curtains. What curtains are left? Get another bedspread. Quick."

After a fleeting search, I concluded that the remains of the dining room and remains of the living room curtains were the only whole matching ones that we could hang in the dinning room. The rest were shredded. *Poor doggie.* "Please, Lord, don't let the lady who gave the house to the church come to visit just now." Katherine was a cool-under-stress and helpful friend. She even managed to get me to laugh a few times.

It took quite a while before we finally could afford to replace the damaged shutters, the patched and mended bedspread and the living room curtains. *Love the doggie, the adorable puppy!*

My supplications regarding the lady who gave the manse were answered. And the college choir ladies sang sublimely that evening even though I conjured malevolent fantasies toward them.

The dog? You'll just have to guess.

Chapter 29
INNOCENT BUT FOUND GUILTY

Any time you are in the public eye there will be those moments of misunderstanding. Innocent, but found guilty. Very disconcerting!

A church secretary was inherited when we arrived at our new church. She was a problem to the church, but the elders were waiting for my husband to arrive to fire her. Isn't that a great way to start our ministry? The major problem was her lack of confidentiality. (A gossip in layman's terms) She also thought it was very creative to change fonts on every paragraph of her letters. I guess to save paper she would type to the very edge of the page. My husband, being very kind, wanting to see if he could make it work...he couldn't.

Where did I enter the picture of this saga? I had been helping the youth leader and he had a brochure he wanted me to do. I didn't want to bother the secretary, so during her lunch hour I typed the flyer for the youth director. Somehow she found out and completely misread my actions.

A month or so later, Roger decided that we really did need a new secretary, the woman just didn't catch on to her problem issues. The elders let her go in as kind of way as they could after giving her two other warnings. A short time later I got a phone call from her son who threatened my life because he knew they fired his mother because I wanted to take over her job. I chuckled to my self, and to assure the woman's son I said, "Of all the people in the world, I would be the most unlikely person to hire as secretary: I hate detail, typing, and sitting, plus the fact I was not going to be the secretary and didn't want to be the secretary. Of course he was still convinced that was the reason she had been fired.

You never know when or where issues like this will pop their ugly heads into your life. Just know these things happen and you are not alone. Again, you just keep loving and hopefully laughing at some of the events that happen in the public eye.

Because of happenings like the above story, I don't jump to conclusions quite as quickly when public figures are condemned for various reasons. I've learned there are always two sides to a story.

"Bear with each other and forgive what ever grievances you may have against one another. Forgive as the Lord forgave you. And over all these virtues put on love which binds them all together in perfect unity."

Chapter 30
THE DEMONS ARE AFTER ME

My mother was born and raised in a wee town in southwestern Scotland called Kilwinin. She, like most of the immigrants who arrived in the States through Ellis Island, brought with her many odd and funny expressions that usually provoked laughter from her children. One of her sayings was, "The demons are after me!" In the midst of any minor frustration she would loudly exclaim that it was that demon causing the problem. One other expression she'd use when she was trying to decipher the obscure directions of a dress making pattern was: "The communists must've written these directions just to frustrate us Americans."

Certainly you've had those demon moments of annoyance with others or yourself.

Several years ago I had one of my *communist* or *demon* moments—actually I've had several. I'm sharing this so that you'll be encouraged when one of your *demon moments* comes.

Roger and I had just arrived at our third church. He was off at his new office while I was busily emptying the boxes of all our earthly goods. Huge and tiny boxes were strewn throughout the house waiting to be unpacked; consequently my frustration level was higher than usual and my spirits were flagging since, so far in our new parish, I had made no new friends. I knew no one. There were no great, generous girlfriends in the neighborhood who would stop by to help.

Why did we have to leave our old parish? In the midst of my funk the phone rang. Where was the phone? I finally found it under some pillows. "Hello," I suspect that my voice was a bit abrupt, but I tried quickly to revert to my best minister's wife sweetness. The caller was a very nice, active and older church member. I met her last Sunday.

"We're all so glad you've come to be with us here. I was just sitting at my kitchen window and thought to myself, "Annabelle, that pretty, young minister's wife probably hasn't a friend in the town since she's so new here and been so busy unpacking. I'll bet she is lonely." So right then I decided that I was going to have a luncheon for you, and I want to introduce you to all my best friends."

I had lived in the South long enough to know this was an important invitation. There was only one response. "Oh, how nice, how thoughtful of you all, I'd just love to come to your home and get to know your friends." With all the unpacking I wondered how I was going to pull it off, but it was a generous invitation, nonetheless. Being fair, many of the younger ladies with kids in school *did* stop by to help and, much to my delight, had exciting decorating suggestions.

After some further chitchat Annabelle and I set a date for Tuesday a week. I added the date in my trusty notebook as we spoke. I hung up and smilingly continued unpacking.

A week later I was still unpacking and greeting church members who dropped by, *just to say hey*; and things were beginning to perk up and look half way presentable. But I was getting worn out. So at about eleven thirty that morning and I had really attacked those pesky boxes, I decided to take a break. I lay on the couch for just a brief moment. Oh, just to close my eyes felt so good. I awoke refreshed and decided to call our daughter, Kathleen to bring her up to date on all the not so interesting unpacking I was doing. We talked and laughed for a long time about her kids and the foibles of my moving into a new community and not knowing anyone—even though I had done it several times before. In the middle of a sentence it struck me, and I shrieked, "Oh my goodness, Kat, I've forgotten my twelve o'clock luncheon invitation. I totally forgot and it's now after one…I'm mortified. What can I do? Say hi to the kids and tell them that grandma loves them." I hung up.

I was so embarrassed I could hardly bring myself to call the very gracious hostess, but I knew I must; not calling would be the end of the town's good will toward their new minister. I fantasized the party's hostess saying to everyone at church: "I don't want to say this, my dear, and I'm sure you'll understand, and, of course, it's in the strictest confidence, and, yes, even though our new minister is from the North he seems nice enough, but, his wife is a ditz. Can you believe, I gave one of my best luncheons and she never showed up?"

Reluctantly, I looked up her number and called. I knew immediately that she was not happy. She said that she had been trying to call me for *an hour*! I tried lamely to explain that I had gotten a call from my Chicago daughter and the time just flew by. Ugh! I sounded bad trying to assuage my guilt. *I knew the demons were after me as my mother jokingly said.* "I am so sorry. Oh, I'm so, so sorry." Turning the knife just a bit more she told me that she had her table decorated ever so prettily, "The ladies loved it and said they'd never seen anything so pretty." The food she described in detail was also beyond delicious—"Everybody went all out to impress the new minister's wife—it was all home cooked and beautiful and all the ladies so much wanted to meet you." I was trying to remember where I had put the unpacked kitchen knives so that I could slash my wrists. Roger was *not* going to be happy. By this time I was one and half hours late and I was hoping everyone had left the party and gone home. But no, Annabelle graciously said I could come over now, but everyone had eaten. *Another turn of the knife* that she did so gently I hardly noticed that I was bleeding profusely.

I couldn't face that situation. Frankly, I didn't want to go to any luncheon that day or ever. I was in paint splashed jeans, my hair was a mess, so decided I *couldn't* go and begged off. Annabelle kept telling me how disappointing this was for her, and I kept saying, "I am so sorry." I tried to explain what had happened, but I was just digging my hole deeper. "Please try to forgive me." "Now, Miss Joy, wasn't that a great way to start out a new ministry in a new town," I admonished myself. Certainly my forgetfulness would become a gossipy magpie that would fly through the aviary of every older woman in town. "Now, my dear, I must tell you this in the strictest confidence...."

Lord, is there anything I can do to make this better, anything?

Each Wednesday evening the church held a family dinner to which most of the congregation attended. I was there. I was the new minister's wife, for Pete's sake! I searched for Annabelle to say, in person, how sorry I was for missing her very gracious luncheon. I could tell she was still upset at me when I found her at a far table. I made an attempt to be conciliatory, crawl through burning coals or clean her house forever. But, instead a thought flashed into my head. Beware of those flashes, they're not always good. But this one had to be from the Lord because it just wasn't my natural inclination. I said to the distraught Annabelle that I wanted to invite her, and all her favorite ladies, to a luncheon at my house. "I really want to meet your friends and to say thank you for your kindness, and try to apologize." Her face lit up somewhat and she agreed. I added, with a gleeful afterthought, "Now y'all don't forget the date."

In preparation for my grand *mea culpa*, I dragged all the boxes from the dinning and living rooms and created my best luncheon *ever*.

Annabelle and I subsequently became good friends after that luncheon (even I was impressed with my water cress petit fours. I even cut the crusts from my best homemade bread). Those gracious Southern ladies adored me. "Honey, where ever did you learn to put on such a magnificent spread? Why it just took me back to when I was a girl."

The demons fled.

Chapter 31
HOW TO GET INTO TROUBLE

Roger and I have been amazed at the delights we have had in our years of ministry. But the *least* delightful church came as a surprise. Perhaps the Lord thought we could handle the bumps in the road by then, or maybe He knew we needed to know how people felt when going through similar tough times. Whatever, we did go through three or four difficult years in the middle of our tenure at a particular church.

If you've ever gone through periods of difficulty in your church, criticisms, misunderstandings from a few vocal people, with no way of dealing with the issue, nor what was really at the root of the problem, keep reading.

During those stressful years, I became preoccupied and stressed trying to think of a hundred solutions. As well, I tried hard not to cause waves in any areas. I often wanted to escape to Kuala Lumpur or an esoteric, enchanting villa just outside Paris.

In the middle of our difficult time, Roger, my always responsible husband, was asked to give the opening prayer one Sunday afternoon at the dedication of a new school library that was to honor an amazing woman, a friend and a faithful member of our church. What was even more remarkable was that Roger was asked to lead the prayer by a church member who was also one of the most disgruntled parishioners, disgruntled mainly because we had started an early morning contemporary worship service. Totally out of character, Roger forgot the event. *Mr. Calendar Man,* who checked his Day-Timer many times each day—forgot the event! At the last bong of our living room tall grandfather clock, at the very moment when Roger was to be at the meeting and invoking God's good graces, the phone rang, a call from Mr. Disgruntled. "Dr. Gulick, do you know where you are supposed to be at *this moment?*" he rasped like the mimic of a disgruntled school marm, shaking her finger at her most disappointing, obviously failing, student.

We lived fifteen minutes away, and it was time for the prayer, NOW. All I wanted to do was die (just after I'd committed homicide), because I knew the implications of Roger's awful moment. So that left Mr. Disgruntled to invoke God's good graces for our friend.

So there would never be any more missed appointments, never happened again, lesson learned. Right? Wrong.

With the coming of Christmas, the staff Christmas party was on our schedule. The party was always on a Friday, usually at our home. But the staff had become too large for that anymore. We loved those times of great holiday food and laughter, exchanging gifts and lots of laughter because there was always a jokester on staff. We would be with our best friends, for that's how we felt about our terrific staff. We wouldn't miss that party for anything.

That year's party was scheduled for Friday evening. Friday was Roger's usual day off. No problem, we didn't need to be reminded that this was the week of the staff party. Roger had the *best party of the year* in his trusty Day-Timer. But, it just so happened that our son and his wife just arrived and we all were out doing some last minute Christmas shopping. I always enjoyed all the lights and tinsel and bustle in all the shops, each trying to out decorate each other. I loved it.

Roger and our son, Tim, had just gone off to look for something special for his wife, Annette. Annette and I, in a festive mood, stopped for a quick meal at a cute little restaurant. We were also looking for a present for Roger. We finally got to browsing in one of the town's nicer men's shops. As I was standing at the counter fingering through ties and wallets and sniffing Ralph Lauren cologne, a thought, like the cologne, wafted into my consciousness. I shouted, "Oh no! Annette, we forgot the church staff Christmas party." *The pastor, head of staff, Mr. Nice Guy, forgot his own Christmas party!* Further, I had no clue where Roger and Tim had gone to shop, so I called the church. Being sanguine, (ruddy faced and cheerful, a psychologist friend of ours told me that), I hated to face anything painful, particularly when we were already going through some tough times and knew that this would add to the very sweet pot of criticism. And anyway, how could anyone forget their own Christmas party! The person on the other end of the phone, shouted, "Joy, where are you and Roger?"

I quickly said, "Roger's in the hospital!"

"Oh no, is that true?"

"No, but I wish he were." He laughed and I said that we were so sorry, mortified actually. So I blamed everything on our missionary kids who had unexpectedly just arrived home and we were having such a great reunion time. We just forgot, we forgot. My voice trailed off. "Will you ever be able to forgive us? We'll be right there." I frantically called Roger wondering where he and Tim were and said very calmly, Roger, dearest. Guess what today is" He pondered for a minute. Silence. "What?"

"Staff Christmas party," I nearly screamed.

"Oh no," was his painful reply! He dashed to the party which was just ending. He did a lame ho, ho, ho. Poor Roger, the senior minister, had to go through the purgatory of embarrassed cheerfulness *alone.* His staff lamely cheered him up, gave him some fruit cake and a gift. And he limped home.

That favorite memory shared by all the staff is always remembered with gales of laughter each time our former staff friends get together.

And be assured that *our* favorite Christmas story became one of the juiciest morsels shared negatively by the Olympic gossipers of the church. Be assured there was always the added addendum: "He didn't care about his people."

I tell you this sad/funny story, because something similar will certainly happen to you, your husband or your kids, and you will be misunderstood. But as one wonderful pastor friend told us, "Time takes care of most things. If you wait, this too shall pass."

Our task was to respond as Christ would have us respond and that takes the transforming power of God.

"If I gave everything to poor people, and if I were burned alive for preaching the gospel but didn't love others, it would be of no value whatsoever" I Corinthians 13:3.

Chapter 32
THE DISGRUNTLED WOMAN

One Sunday I was sitting in Roger's office. A regular and active church member walked in to complain about something. Whatever it was, she was angry and wanted the Senior Minister to know about it. After she finished talking to Roger, who seemed to have the gift of calming her down, she looked over at me and said, "And you, every time you walk down the hall on Sundays and you see me, you turn your head, stick your nose in the air and ignore me." "A nice, gentle person like me? Me? You must have someone else in mind," I thought.

I hadn't a clue what she was talking about. In my most understanding voice I explained, "That's just not something I would do—to anyone." I lamely tried to explain that sometimes when I'm preoccupied with some event or other that I'm in charge of, I become unaware of what is going on around me. "But, I *do* apologize." She was not convinced. I was thinking of slashing my wrists but doubted if that would appease that very unhappy woman. Who knows how many people our disappointed parishioner told: "That minister's wife just ignores me? I don't like her." One cannot do anything about that. But there is something we can do.

When misunderstandings happen, I try to follow the advice the mother of an old boyfriend gave me, "Just love 'em into loveliness." As I acted on that advice I sensed that, perhaps, healing would finally come for that angry woman. Know that people who want recognition from leadership in the church can read a negative into almost anything said or not said, done or not done. Don't let it get you down; just ask God to help you reach out to them in love and ask Him to deal with it.

Chapter 33

SOMETIMES IT'S FOGGY OUT THERE

Our son, Tim, was in the middle of his high school junior year. He loved it, partly because the school was an excellent example of a great private school, but, and especially, he had a girlfriend. Ah, the happy life of Spring and love.

But, wouldn't you know, a little glitch appeared in our bucolic household. Roger was called to a new church. Oh my, the whole family had conflicted prayers about the decision, but wisely Roger and I knew Roger's call had to be a call for the entire family. Too many rebellious preachers' kids' stories circle around parishes.

Happily our kids were fairly flexible–as much as teenagers can manage– and were accepting of the move; but Roger and I knew this was not going to be an easy move for them since they had spent all of their school years in one town. Needless to say, Tim had extremely mixed feelings about the move.

After the ardors of packing and a nail biting move in a blizzard, and for the kids a whole new life in the middle of the school year, the bleakness of the move struck—unfamiliar manse, cold, grey town, no friends, lots of long distance phone calls back *home,* unpacking, "Where should I put this?", there was sadness. What had we done?

For Tim, the discovery of a not so good public school, cultural differences, no close friends, and seven hours by car from his girlfriend became his silent anguish. Happily, the youth group was good and we were impressed that Tim was trying valiantly to deal with all the changes. But soon he was just sitting in his room, slumped over his desk while studying. His whole body bespoke sadness.

Not Kathleen. She reveled in her new co-ed high school, received A's without trying and became involved in all the extra curricular activities she could find: student council, soccer, tennis, and anything and everything else. She loved it. She was the new girl in town! Thank you, Lord.

The move continued to be hard for Tim. We felt sure he would adjust. We even thought it might be good for him to go through this struggle and learn life lessons while we were there to support him. We were wrong about that, but we did understand his struggles. We knew them intimately; we were pretty much at the same place.

Then, one day, good friends from our former church called with a very kind, creative, and unexpected offer. "Why don't you let Tim come live with us for his senior year?" We knew Tim would love it, (his face really lit up with the idea) but we hated to give up having him around, and our missing his senior year of high school. Were we being unrealistic and totally selfish about keeping him with us? But as usual, we prayed and talked, and prayed some more. It was a heart and mind and spirit struggle. The more we prayed, the more we thought we should let Tim go to live with a wonderful family in our old, familiar neighborhood. Enjoy your senior year, Tim. We'll visit. Tim was very excited and it turned out we made the right decision.

The following summer Tim happily came home and got a job as life guard at the local country club. It was a wonderful time having him with us before he went off to college.

Be comforted. Know, as you seek God's will, that you will be directed on *your* path, and your children will grow up well and emotionally strong when they know their parents are with them—even though, sometimes, just for a while, it will be like walking reluctantly through a fog.

Chapter 34
YOU CAN DO IT

I never kept a personal calendar. I was always ready for anything in a moment's notice—particularly if fun was involved. I sailed through my younger years like a brave and adventuresome yachter with a brisk breeze at my back; I was excellent at multitasking after my eleven summers of imposed waitress duties at my parent's restaurant. I was a pro.

Flexibility and sanguinity were great—and saved me—when I was young and single and had little to worry about other than remembering *stupid* math formulas or whether I'd ever have a date with that hunk of a guy I'd just seen on the beach.

Then along came my lovable clergy husband and his schedule, my active children's demands (yes, yes we'll go next week), their school activities, their interminable seasonal sports, church schedules with the ever present meetings and dinners and decorating and praying, and, oh, yes, my own activities, wash my hair, clean the house, cook breakfast and dinner. Phew!

It abruptly occurred to me one day (It took me far too long.) that I planned two events for the same day at the same time and that I also had just plain missed two important events that I really wanted to go to. Not Good!

"My dear, have you noticed our minister's wife seems so scattered, running about trying to be into everything? Does she drink?"

Lots of embarrassments. I hated that part of being a sanguine. I apologized profusely and frequently when I forgot or missed something important such as a wedding or funeral or even a fun party. My *irresponsibility* needed to be fixed! Now. After all, I WAS a minister's wife. Get it together, girl.

God in his graciousness, helped by Roger, scheduled a speaker and his wife at our church. The husband was a well known speaker around the country; she was Anne Ortland, author of *"The Disciplines of a Beautiful Woman."* Since I was the clergy-wife entertainer for the special guest speaker for the weekend, she and I had extra time just to talk—clergy wife to clergy wife. I off-handedly mentioned my "forgetting."

"Oh, I know what you mean." Then she added, she, the wiser, older, gracious woman, "You just need to get yourself a small pocketbook that included a scheduling pages, (The wonderful new version of this idea is the iphone, which at that time had not even been thought of). I carry mine all the time."

A red flag went up. I swallowed a laugh by putting the rest of the brownie we had just cooked in my mouth. *Carry it with me all the time!* That'll never happen

The clever response of the older woman was said very knowingly without a hint of condescension, "I know it'll just take a little bit of discipline to always carry a notebook with you. But you'll get on to it."

She continued, "In your notebook you have to have: A yearly calendar, a weekly calendar, all your addresses and phone numbers. Then you'll need a section for each committee you're on and space for note taking. All you'll ever need to know will be with you all the time. So, if someone asks you to dinner or a meeting, just whip out your trusty note book (or iphone) and see if, perchance, there is a conflict."

She added that I will have to look at my schedule every morning when I get up. The big hurdle would be whether I was that disciplined? Could I do it? Sure. I was desperate.

I carried a newly purchased notebook every day for a month. It was my "alter your behavior" activity period. Simple!

I did it! By the end of the month that lil' ole black book had become my constant companion, and it kept its promise to save me from the further embarrassments of missing or conflicting appointments.

The notebook/pocketbook was life changing. Not only did it keep me from problems, it gave me a sense of peace and equanimity, knowing that I could find and anticipate my daily activities right there. Freedom! Occasionally I still smile about and secretly miss my sanguine self that frantically looked for that little sticky note with Mary's phone number on it that I knew was somewhere in the house. Not to worry, I'll find it; it'll only take me a minute.

Chapter 35

YOUR HUSBAND-
YOUR PREACHER

I remember wondering when we were invited to our first church what it would be like listening to my husband preach every Sunday. What if I didn't like his sermons? After all, in the past I had heard some of the country's best preachers. Would I be so nervous that I couldn't be ministered to? If Roger really bombed, where would I hide? I concluded that I'd just pretend I liked it—so much for trust in God's faithfulness.

Much to my delight, as soon as Roger stood to speak, he became my pastor and I was ministered to. But there *were* two times in Roger's thirty-eight years of preaching that I had a different reaction: Once I was listening to his sermon and becoming more and more annoyed at what he was saying. He was too direct and insensitive; the sermon was awful and I was angrier at him than the situation called for. I could hardly wait for the service to be over to ask him what in the world happened. I wanted to say, "You were terrible this morning." Why was I was so upset?

When the service was finally over the woman sitting in front of me turned around and had tears in her eyes and said, "That was the best sermon I have ever heard."

One other time I had that extreme reaction and again the person in front of me turned with tears in her eyes and said that was the most meaningful sermon she had ever heard.

I began to ponder what was happening to me (was I menopausal?) and I wondered why, when I got upset at Roger's sermon, the same thing happened. I concluded that God was using Roger in significant ways and perhaps the devil was attacking me. My reaction was certainly bazaar.

I recommend that if an unexplained upset happens to you, begin praying for your husband. God is possibly using him in new ways. I might be wrong about this, but at least consider the idea. Another possibility for this happening was that I was being taught again that even in our weaknesses (or my husband's weakness) He (God) is made strong.

Another thought that helps with the issue of my preacher husband, is that if God has called him to the ministry, God will be faithful in using him and his gifts and empowering him for his task. Our job is to pray and encourage and **sometimes** carefully give a few hints on how he could improve. But watch the timing of your comments. My Young Life director, Jerry Johnson always told me when I was on staff, that I was never to correct a Young Life Leader's talk right after he or she spoke, because at that point they would be too emotionally involved to be objective. Wait a day.

A good suggestion for pastors' wives.

Chapter 36
BOUNDARIES

Because Roger was associate pastor in our second church, he was in charge of the young adults, college and career, and high school groups; I had the opportunity to work with him on many of those activities. We had two children and were committed to be there with them as much as we could. The four of us always ate together for breakfast and dinner. During breakfast we would read great books to them.: C.S. Lewis's Chronicles of Narnia, the Bible, or what ever was a good read.

When Roger and I went out at night to lead small groups at a friend's home, we would have a baby sitter who would arrive after the children were in bed. In those instances when we went to a high school camp, the children went along. Those camps were some of their best memories. But, because I loved all my work, well most of it, and loved my children and our church activities, I kept taking on more and more assignments. One year, I taught a senior high Sunday school class, sang in the choir, attended three couple's small groups a week that Roger led, and had breakfast at our house for 30 junior high students each Wednesday morning. After our children were in bed on Saturday night we created a Coffee House at the church for senior high students. We also had a Sunday night youth group. I also had just been made chair woman of the city's *Christian Women's Club*—a huge undertaking. And I led two young women's Bible studies.

Because I loved all I was doing, I thought I could do it all, plus keep a house and cook three meals a day, with no ill effect. I was just having fun. Too frequently there would be a troubled college student (usually boy/girl stuff that the student felt demanded instant attention, lest they die) that I counseled with—often till one in the morning. Then I had to get up at a bone-weary hour to feed the kids and Roger.

Finally, my body started sending alarm signals, to which I paid no attention. But increasingly I couldn't sleep—*that had never been a problem before.* Of course, I ignored the signs. Oh yes, wild, frightening nightmares began. I was depressed and denied it, I just wanted to sleep and sleep. That wasn't like me, so I just kept pushing. Of course, I prayed for God to lift whatever was bugging me, but He seemingly ignored my distracted requests because He knew I needed to learn about creating boundaries around my time.

"Roger, I think I need to back out of some things I've committed myself to." Distractedly he said, "Oh, sure, OK, whatever you want.." I hadn't shared with him my horrible feeling: Christians are not supposed to be depressed. But I did drop out of choir and the youth groups. I began taking long walks and I even went to our doctor to see if he could find anything physically wrong. Nothing!

My depression was not fun, to say the obvious. I read good books and medical texts that tried to explain depression, for now I had time, that precious commodity. I slowly began to realize that my intense joy in working with youth and with Roger had sapped my physical and spiritual strength. I began saying, when people asked me to take on a new chore, "Give me some time to pray about it." Then I would pray and look at my schedule realistically and talk to Roger to see what he thought. One day, very tentatively, I asked Roger if he thought it would be possible, *just possible*, if we could afford to have someone come in to help me clean, just every other week, or so, for a couple of hours. (My prayer group put me up to it.) He wonderfully said, "Sure, why not." That was the best thing ever that helped me play catch up, and got me off my self inflicted and relentless treadmill.

Now, I am really *thankful* for those two months of situational depression. They're gone now! Good bye forever. Not only did I learn to set my own boundaries, but I began to understand in new ways what depression feels like. I became more sympathetic and understanding. Before that I probably would have thought, when someone told me they were depressed, "Buck up. Pull yourself together, for Pete's sake"…or at least thought it. It was also a great insight to discover that some depressions are biochemical in nature and can only be helped by the appropriate medications. (Be sure to see your physician if you are concerned.) And reaffirm that what God takes us through is never wasted. In my case, many depressed people sought me out to talk about *their* depression. Talking it out for some was helpful. Someone was there who understood. Be sure also to build good checks and balances in your life, use your husband or a woman friend to frankly help you stop running on your own steam, and stop trying to conquer the world.

Chapter 37
SUBTLE
PRESSURES

Pressure, often subtle—often blatant—can haunt pastors and their wives.

Our car was getting older; no it was old, really old. Miles had accrued from our twelve hour traipsing to vacation spots, to and from family homes, and seventeen hour treks to Illinois for equal parent-time vacations. Then there were the many drop offs ("please Mother, please!") of our children for after school track, and gymnastics, and tennis lessons, and church youth groups ("It's raining!"). Our grumbling, weary Chevy required more and more visits to the local garage, causing *money to fly out our windows*—and we had a lot of windows.

"Rog, honey, do you think it's time for us to, maybe, possibly look for a new car" I said as off handedly and nonchalantly as possible for I didn't want a, *but the Chevy only has 120,000 miles on it* response.

Roger, as I've said, has a remarkably mathematical mind, honed by his engineer training; he was insistent about looking into all the obscure statistics for every car ever built—their price, colors, mpg's and, I don't know what all, but he researched. Then, as we always did, we prayed about using money wisely, especially since we didn't have very much. Then, of course, our standard practice was always (well almost always) to agree on any major purchase. "God, give us wisdom as we search and decide." He always did.

It just so happened (not really a surprise) that there was a car salesman in one of our small groups. Joe now became our expert counselor on motor vehicles. "Sure, I'll look through our inventory for good secondhand car for you." (Is there such a thing?)

About a month later our now *best, best friend and car salesman* said that he had a great three year old Audi—good price, great condition, beautiful color, leather seats, all the gadgets, $10,300. We didn't know at the time that Joe had talked his boss into selling the car for only $300 profit for the car, instead of the $2,000 they might have made. All our previous cars had been gadgetless. Leather seats, what were they? (I'm trying to impress you with how holy I was.) Plus, that car, after we zoomed around the neighborhood, *trying it out* on the highway, drove like a cloud. Being totally trusting, and just in case, Roger followed the *Consumer Report's* guidelines, we had another garage checkout the car. All was well. "It's *a steal.*" We bought it. It *was* a cloud. We and the kids loved it.

Now the subtle, (like prayers) spoken and unspoken, often whispered responses from the saintly parishioners. I don't know if anyone actually thought theses things, but I couldn't stop thinking they might.

Hmm, how can *they* afford a car like that, *my dear*?

Where's he getting *that* kind of money…an Audi! Can you believe it?

My dear, they're certainly very materialistic, seems to me, very worldly. It just breaks my heart.

We can't afford a car like *that,* how does he do it on a minister's salary?

My whole being wanted to put a sign on the back of our new car—over the license plate—saying:

WE ONLY PAID $10,300 FOR THIS CAR!

WE'RE SO SORRY THAT WE HAVE SUCH A NICE CAR!

HAVE A NICE DAY.

GOD BLESS YOU!

It's important to fight the demons of gossip. Rather say, "We prayed and did what we felt was right. Thank you, Lord, for a wonderful gift." Unfortunately, there wasn't enough room on our license plate for all my wild feelings. But truth is, no matter what a clergy family does, some glorious parishioner can complain or feel exceptionally self-righteous because they have a Chevy. *"I thank God that I am not as others with their big cars."*

"Christ committed no sin when insults were hurled at him. He did not retaliate...He made no threats. He entrusted himself to Him who judges justly."

I Peter 2: 22-23

Chapter 38
LEAVING CHURCHES

I don't know of a church where Roger pastored that, when the time came, wasn't a struggle to leave. I had so many wonderful relationships to say goodbye to, a home to leave and a comfort zone to upset, plus a place where our children had become entrenched.

When we left our first church, I cried uncontrollably as we drove away. The second church we left, I cried a bit, but half way down the road I pulled myself together. By the third church, I was laughing and waving *as we drove out of sight.* I had discovered from experience that each move to a new church brought many things new that I would not have wanted to miss, nor could have anticipated.

In one of our early churches, everyone my age had to work, due to the difficult economic circumstances of the area. Consequently, for me there was no one during the week that I could get together with. Gritting my teeth, I reluctantly learned to be alone, not one of my strongest gifts.

However, because of all my free time I decided to take voice lessons again, (I used to be pretty good) and would practice three hours a day. Whatever *your* unique circumstances, use them creatively.

At the same church, the last three years, the Lord gave me one of my best friends ever, a soul mate. (That's important to us people persons.) However, the next church we went to was one of our harder churches…at the same time very exciting. The church had gone through many hurts: a split in the church, (they are one of those inglorious events that plague congregations—my team is right, yours is out of God's will), and a pastor who had an affair with a member of the congregation. The congregation, *the bride of Christ*, went through what was equivalent to a divorce from an unfaithful husband.

When we arrived on the scene the leaders and those in the congregation were very nervous about ministers in general. They looked under every stone to discover whether they could trust us, making for some very difficult times for Roger and me. We were scrutinized closely; consequently Roger went through some rough times. While he was struggling, I kept itching to fix it, but I had no idea what needed to be fixed. I prayed, but peace eluded me. I prayed for three years: nothing changed.

One day I was studying Joshua in the Old Testament. Joshua was in one of those, "fit the battle of Jericho" moments when God said: "Stand still and see the deliverance of the Lord." It struck me, all too belatedly, that the situation in the church was not my battle, nor even Rogers, but God's. I began contemplating what was the worst thing that could happen to us? They could fire Roger, toss us both on one of those rag-a-muffin, shabby chic, Carolina beaches. That was unlikely, but whether we stayed as senior pastor or left, I realized it would not be the end of the world. It was under His care and control. *Be Still. Discover my deliverance.* A peace came over me that could only have been from God, and I never was anxious about that situation again. Within a week God removed a family who was one of the keys to the problem. God was teaching me a new lesson of trust. He didn't let up until I got an A grade with that lesson. Again, after sixteen years, as hard as it was to leave, I realized that through those difficulties God had taught us lots of lessons that we would need for our retirement years of pastoring missionary families. As we left that church, I was excited about the new adventures God had in store. Emotionally I realized finally, leaving churches was not the end, but the beginning of a new exciting adventure with Him.

"For I know the plans I have for you", declares the Lord, "plans to prosper you and not harm you, plans to give you a future and a hope" Jeremiah 29: 11.

Chapter 39
EXPECTATIONS

Yet another tricky issue that arises for ministers wives is that members often have impossible expectations. There are church members who want you just to be quiet, please just stay in the background, thank you. Conversely, you will be expected by others to be outgoing, bright, clever, articulate, almost a second pastor. (To say nothing of your children.) As well, there are those who want you to be a fashion plate and others who want you to look plain and muted. "My dear that outfit is so attractive. Did you get it at the thrift store?" All these expectation can be in one church and of course can cause clashes in expectations. It was important for me, and so for you, to figure out what it is God wants us to be, to do or not do. I discovered my focus needed to be on whom the Lord created me to be and what He wanted me to do. Any other way will lead to frustration as when we try to please one church person, we too often will displease another.

One example of this resulted from my having been a Christian Education major in college and in graduate school. I loved serving voluntarily in different capacities. In one church I was on the Christian Education Committee, worked with small groups, and was in choir. My children had grown and were in college, thus I had free time and I loved serving in those capacities.

One day an elder came up to me in the hall of the church and said that the church committees had been re-structured and I was no longer to be on the Christian Education Committee. That was it, thank you, ma'am and goodbye.

No explanation was made. I was shocked. "Did I do something wrong?" I called after him as he strolled off down the hall.

"Oh, no!" he shouted over his shoulder. I knew that in this particular church they were afraid that a minister's wife would have too much influence. Apparently the former pastor's wife was considered a negative, overwhelming influence (some of us can be like that) and they didn't want that to happen again.

My friend, the Christian Education Director said to me, "Joy, the former pastor's wife ruined it for you." You will never know what you are walking into in a new church. The extra time I had by not serving on the Christian Education Committee led me to volunteer with *Habitat for Humanity's* Selection and Nurture Committee. God used the angry fears of some of the parishioners for good in my life—even though it hurt at the time. "*I am a firm believer that the LORD sometimes has to SHORT CIRCUIT even our best plans for our benefit.*" Tony Dungy

In case you're getting the idea that minister's wives have to be highly involved in their husband's ministry, let me assure you that that is not true. In my case, I just happened to have certain gifts and talents to offer and was delighted in doing so. Each minister's wife is different, and God's call on her life is different. The important things to remember:

1. Desire to be Christ's person wherever He calls you.

2. Do all you do as a gift to the Lord—not just because someone asks or it's your profession. Share your gifts out in the community if there is strife, or meanness or jealousy in your congregation.

3. Know that God can take our inadequacies or strengths and accomplish what He desires. That's true for all God's people.

Chapter 40
FUNERALS

Part of a clergy wife's activities, chores, or adventures is attending funerals. But they too include some subtle learning experiences. For instance: what in the world does one say to a wife whose husband has died after forty years of marriage or to a newlywed whose husband dies in a car crash; or to a mom whose two year old child dies from a fatal fall? We, the true help mate of our pastor-husband, need to know what to do or say.

As a newly wed, my first real experience with death–up-close and personal couldn't have been worse...I'm still embarrassed.

Two weeks after we were married, Roger, had to return to sea duty for a six months' cruise. We had been married for just two weeks and now I was very alone. In the quaint (beyond bleak that winter) New England town, I fortunately made friends with other officer's wives through a church Bible study. I was a first year, bumbling school teacher. I had a new marriage, new job, and had no idea what I had gotten myself into. Romance, far away places? Forget about them. It was bleak and lonely. During those first six months, however, I did befriend a great Christian girl, Betty, another navy wife who had five little ones to care for. Her husband, Bob, was an engineer working on the USS Thresher, a new atomic submarine. He had just left for a shakedown cruise that would see how well the boat was working.

Something went terribly wrong on their first day out. A valve failed, water rushed in and sunk the boat and at that depth the Thresher was crushed. Every man was lost. The national media went ballistic; there was grieving and alarm that carried way beyond our salty little costal town.

In the navy, when husbands are on sea duty for long periods of time there always develops a close bond between the wives left in home port. They take care of and look out for each other. It's really very wonderful.

The news of the Thresher's catastrophic implosion came over the television just after I had arrived at Betty's small apartment for coffee. I was thrust into the middle of the biggest crisis Betty would ever have; I was overwhelmed with the horror of the situation, clueless as to what to say or do. I began to make mindless blunders. (The only person who had died in my family was a distant grandmother. I was too young even to be taken to her funeral.) Being the off-spring of my mother's Scottish heritage where one seldom showed affection or caring through touching, I was next to useless. The overwhelming shock of the event was too much for me to offer a simple, caring hug. I should have hugged Betty and cried with her. Instead I talked and talked, almost a jabber. I asked, what in retrospect, were stupid, misplaced questions. (Remember: timing is everything.) "What are you going to do now?" I asked trying to be sympathetic. (How could she know?) "Do you think you'll remarry? How sad for me and my clueless inexperience. Little did I know then that no words were needed. You, in your new position will be thrown into all kinds of funeral situations, and if you have an inkling of what to do, that will help. Start out with being genuinely caring. With church members you don't know very well, possibly a hug and, "I am so sorry," or "I will be praying for you."

It's a tad different if the wife has died and you're in the business of comforting the widower. Age makes a difference: If the bereaved husband is eighty, a hug and kind words will be helpful. Otherwise a warm handshake and a few words of sympathy are what is needed.

With close friends you need to be there with them. Many words are usually not needed. Just be there for them to talk with you about whatever they need to talk about. Your presence in the days and weeks that follow will mean a lot and helping with details like coordinating food for family and relatives, answering the door when all the people arrive at their home with food or a greeting. But just showing up and being with the bereaved and letting them take the lead in what they want to talk about is the best.

Each person is different in terms of presence. Some need more support, others need space. When you know them well, you merely ask them if they would like you to be there. Read body language as well as their words. Some people just don't want to bother you, but wish you would be there. (I'm shouting here: DoNOT GO TO A WIDOWER'S HOUSE ALONE.) At least take a girlfriend. Going with your husband you would be just fine.

Rejoice with those who rejoice: mourn with those who mourn. *Romans 12:15*

Chapter 41
CHURCH CULTURES

Mores! What are they? "Oh, it's just the way we do things around here." Be assured, every church has them. Sometime before you learn what your church's expectations or right way of doing things are, you can bungle some big ones before you have a clue what's going on.

For example: In the northeastern part of our country, church members generally went to their own family funerals. One typically attended their parents, grandparents, cousins, aunt and uncles' funerals. If a close friend died one attended that funeral, but seldom would you attend your friend's grandparent's uncle's funeral, unless, of course you knew the relative very well.

Not so in the southern part of our country. In one of our southern churches, for instance, one *must* attend every member of your church's funeral—even your church friend's family, even if they lived out of town and you had never met them. This custom, we belatedly discovered, was very important to everyone and showed proper respect. If you were born in this cultural tradition—no problem. You would just know the right thing to do. We didn't.

A friend and member of the church during the first two years at our new church had been very kind and generous with us. "Joy, why don't you and Roger, go on down to our beach house next Thursday on your day off. Nobody'll be there." *The little beach house* was a lovely, grey shingled place, conveniently located just along the surf with every amenity color coordinated. You can count on the fact that we motored on down to that *cottage* the very next Thursday.

The beach house owner's ninety-five year old grandmother, whom we had never met nor even heard of—up and died. She lived at least two hours away. It never entered our minds that we were expected to attend the funeral. Roger had not been asked to officiate since the mother was not a member of our church. When we heard of the death, we called the family and offered our sympathies. Since no invitation had been offered, we never gave it a thought that we were expected to be there. Oh, we were so wrong! Sadly our friendship with the beach house owners cooled off greatly, as much as I tried to explain, never to recover. And, no, we did not often get asked to return to that lovely, grey shingled place, conveniently located, just along where the surf playfully splashes.

Another expectation: If one is really a *good* pastor's wife, one bakes bread from a Betty Crocker Cook-off, first place recipe (preferably a recipe from before the War between the States that was passed down from our Aunt Pittipat) and takes the still warm bread to people in the church who are hurting or struggling or dying or are new in the community. I'd never done that, nor heard of the tradition—nor wanted to. When first moving in I had been told of the custom while I was hauling a huge carton off the moving van and into our empty, echoing, new manse. "Aggie Johnston has just lost her husband; He was the editor of the newspaper. I think it would be wise for you to take her some of your best, home-baked bread." I smiled and thanked Ms. What's-Her-Name, and called Roger to help me lift our huge arm chair and move it into the house—as she looked on. Well in the hustle and bustle of moving I forgot the regional expectation. I shouldn't have! And I regret it. I had problems from day one with that *lovely* woman ever since. She was a leader of the women of the church. *Live and learn.*

What never dawned on our women's leader-lady was that my tradition was as valid as hers and her local custom. My custom was, as soon as I got the drapes all hung, to have all sorts of people, members and non members, to our home for a meal or invite various people to just stop by for coffee and a dessert. But now I know about the bread custom. It's kind of nice, actually.

In our family's tradition, way back then (I mean, *way* back), to be invited to a pastor's home would have been beyond expectation. But, having gotten accustomed to the "new ways," I loved inviting people for dinner. It helped built bridges with people. Jesus seemed to like the custom as well, for so many of his stories tell of his sharing a meal with new friends. Hosting a meal for me was and is fun. And if it is your gift, do it.

Beginning the ministry at one church, each week Roger and I invited the *whole* congregation for dessert—in groups of twenty at a time. It was creative fun, and I thought very clever. But, of course, one lavender dressed lady very stooped from her osteoporosis, irritably asked, "Now, Rev'end Gulick, when are you going to come visit our home for a pastoral call?" It was more important for her that Roger would go to her home to talk about how long they had been members... way back to Aunt Julia. So much for getting it right.

I share these stories so when you *don't* get it right you can learn to privately laugh and realize there are many who went before you who didn't get it right either. All we clergy wives need to do is be the individual, unique person God called us to be and not try to meet every whim and expectation of the congregation. Of course, love demands sensitivity to peoples needs, but He has made each of us with different gifts and temperaments. Pleasing our Lord is what counts.

HOW TO HANDLE UNREALISTIC EXPECTATIONS?

1. Know your unique gifts and work through those. Re-read I Corinthians 12.

Rediscover that not all of us have the same gifts.

Reread Ephesians 4.

Rediscover that not all of us are called to do the same task. And we, sure as shootin', don't need to fret over that.

2. Know that you are never going to meet *everyone's* expectations—

Didn't Jesus get away to a secluded place to pray even when he could have continued teaching or healing the people? He even occasionally had to get away from the throng to be renewed and talk with the Father.

3. You will not be loved by everyone—Jesus wasn't. Don't fret over it.

Chapter 42
FRIENDSHIPS

Can you have friends in the church where your husband is ministering? This is an issue that gets discussed a lot among pastors' wives with arguments falling on both sides. I contend for the "Yes" answer. "You can have friends in the church." It would possibly be easier if you had friends outside the church because you can share your struggles more openly, but the fact of the matter is you spend so much time in the church and at meetings and events, there is hardly any time for outside friendships. We need friendships just like anyone else and need community just like everyone else, and if you can't have friends in the church you will become very lonely and I think that is unrealistic and frankly stupid.

He is your friend who pushes you nearer to God.
Abraham Kuyper, 1837-1920
Misfortune tests the sincerity of friends
Robert E. Lee, 1807-1870
Greater love hath no man than this, that he lay
down his life for his friends.
Jesus Christ, John 15:13
A real friendship is shown in times of trouble;
prosperity is full of friends.
Abraham Kuyper, 1837-1920

Here are some things I did to try to keep my church friendships from causing me trouble.

1. I usually didn't sit with my friends in church very often, but spent time at church trying to get to know as many people as possible. I would go to my friends home to visit or they would come to my home, or go out for coffee or lunch.

2. You have to choose your friends wisely. Friends you can trust with confidentiality. I tried to keep away from discussions about church issues, particularly controversial issues or anything that I happened to know about what the church board was doing, thinking or planning. Sometimes I wanted to give my point of view or tell how stupid I thought something was or how they needed to vote for certain issues, but this was my friend's church, and I didn't want to ruin her church experience, worship or attitudes toward people. Another area where we as pastors' wives have to trust God is for the outcome on issues in the church. As tempting as it is there should be no manipulation on issues or trying to get your friends to vote a certain way. We have to remember we have more information about people and situations than most people in the church and confidentiality is extremely important or it can ruin your husband's opportunity to minister to the church leaders and to people of the congregation who could be hurt if that information got out. Being a sanguine, I am a very open person and share my life pretty freely, but I've had to learn that that is not the case for a lot of people. Things I didn't think were private are very private to others. Confidentiality is crucial. I can't stress that enough.

Prayer is our agent of change not manipulation. I wasn't always successful in carrying this out, but I tried to never manipulate, even subtly.

A prudent man keeps his knowledge to himself, but the heart of fools blurts out folly.   *Proverbs 12:23*
Avoid a man who talks too much.
Proverbs 23:18

Chapter 43
HELPS FOR MARRIAGE

Both my husband and I would say the best thing that ever happened for our marriage and family was attending "Marriage and Family" enrichment conferences. We attended one almost every other year until our children were almost off to college. Either we went to these conferences at other locations or we planned them for our church so all the congregation could participate.

The conferences were so great because they put my husband and me on the same page in our thinking about marriage and raising children. The conferences also saved a lot of years of struggling .We were able to hear other couples laughing at the same life situations that we were now struggling with, which relieved the idea that we were the only ones struggling with a specific area.

A real plus when the conference included small groups was the chance to ask questions of the teachers or other couples who were a few years ahead of us in marriage and family situations. Everyone struggles with their marriage and with their families at some points and it is so nice to have help along the way especially in a very non- threatening setting.

TRY IT YOU'LL LIKE IT.

Chapter 44
A
RECOMMENDATION

All people, I hope, would want to have a good perspective on life. Often living in America we can quickly miss the big picture or get the wrong perspective. Even we, the informed pastors' wives, can loose perspective. We can fall into the trap of thinking such things as: Our income is pretty small and it is hard to keep up with the things we need let alone want. Poor us. Don't people realize we are working hard and making pittance? I would like to get a new dress and I can't, we need a new car and our television is about to die. Our kids want to go to camp and we just don't have the money, etc. That kind of thinking can creep into our minds without us realizing it.

Something that can help remedy that wrong perspective is to seek out an opportunity to go on a mission trip to a two-third's world country. It makes our poor in America look rich in comparison and us very rich indeed.

Roger and I had a chance to go to Africa. What we saw stunned us. We visited the largest slum in the world. There were a million people living in tin or cardboard shacks. The shacks were the size of one of America's walk in closets. Often some of these shacks had eight family members living in them. The floors were of dirt and there were no bathrooms or running water in their homes. A million people!

Running down the middle of the dirt road between the houses was a very narrow stream of sewage with paper, and junk and feces. I felt like I was going to get a disease just walking down the street.

All of a sudden I got a new perspective.

How rich we are! How could I complain? Then I started thinking, how can I get rid of some of my stuff to help the poor and needy? Forgive me, Lord, for my complaining. Instead of thinking, "How can I get more", I began thinking how can I give to people in real need. But, how quickly, especially living in our comfortable situation, I can forget my new perspective and resolutions. So, if you are like me and need a new perspective, try a mission trip, and if you then begin to forget how well you have it, go on another one. It can do wonders.

There are times when you live in an area where the cost of living is higher than your amount coming in for salary. In these cases check your budget carefully to see if there is anything that is unnecessary that could be cut out. If after checking your finances and you are still lacking your husband should go to your churches Elders, Deacons, or whoever your church's leadership is. Kindly show him or them your expenses compared to your salary. Usually they will see the problem and accommodate. If they don't see the financial problem you need to begin praying about your next steps.

My husband had to do that at our first church and their response was very positive and immediate. Thank you, Lord.

Chapter 45
THE DILEMMA

As the *Fiddler on the Roof*'s Tevia exasperatedly tried to explain his dilemmas about life's contradictions, he summed it all up with the phrase, "On the one hand." He'd then see that his life circumstances weren't just one straightforward proposition, for there was always his: "On the other hand." In that same vein, Michael Jendrzejczyk, (*Christian Century,* February 7-14, 1979, p. 151.) astutely identified clergy wives changing and contradictive roles when he wrote in his article, "Whatever Happened to Ministers' Wives?"

First, a description of this endangered species: she seldom worked outside the home unless she was a teacher or nurse. She worried about making financial ends meet, but she was very careful not to mention this preoccupation outside the parsonage bedroom. She was the last to surrender the hat and the white gloves she had always worn to church. She felt guilty if she did not sing in the choir, attend all women's meetings and teach Sunday school. She felt guilty that she was not a good enough Christian to be an exemplary person for one and all. She feared being criticized almost more than she feared death. She tried to be the perfect mother. She was highly embarrassed if any of her brood behaved badly. She tried to be the perfect wife and to do all the things perfect wives did superbly—ironing, cooking, entertaining ad nauseam. She was uptight and believed that that was the only way to be.

Now the few wives who find themselves described as "endangered" may be embarrassed. It is like hearing one's children ask: "Mom how was it in the olden days when you were young?" It wasn't all that long ago, and we weren't all that peculiar. We tried to live as best we could where we were. A lot has happened to us and around us—so much, in fact, that we do not even talk about it among ourselves very often. But let's try.

No doubt the women's movement and the resultant rise in consciousness of women as people have had a great impact on the wives of ministers. In fact many of them were in the forefront of the movement. Nowadays one feels positively guilty if one does not have a career or a job outside the home. One feels downright put upon if one has to prepare all the meals, if one takes care of the children full-time, if one has to entertain often. Somehow one feels that one is deserting one's sisters—and, even worse, setting a rotten example for one's sons and daughters. A new life style is upon us, with new demands, new guilts and, one hopes, new satisfactions. The new woman in the parsonage is having an effect on the way her minister husband feels about life and on the way in which he ministers. One way of looking at this impact is in terms of what this new wife is concerned about and how she is dealing with problems.

Then the *Minister's Wife's* article goes on to describe the numerous hurdles and positives of this new way of thinking and living in the parish house with such subtitles as: Holding Your Marriage Together, Possible Effects on Ministry, Relationships with Children, Insisting on Sharing Labor in the Home, Husband Prefers Housework to His Pastoral Duties, Wife's Career—Refusing to Move When Her Husband Must Move.

ON THE OTHER HAND

As Christians, as women, our societal and feminine norms have changed; but we are under an authority other than our desires, needs and wants or a fickle congregation's wants—bless them. As always, we are primarily obedient to the authority of God and his Word. Isn't it true that most

Sundays in most churches we pray our most familiar prayer: *Our Father, who art in heave, hallowed be Thy name. Thy kingdom come, Thy will be done...*which clearly means we acknowledge that we are not just a minister's wife, but, foremost and finally, we, like all Christians, are followers of Christ. We have pledged our life to his service. That's the starting point. Now it's simply,

> *Trusting in the Lord with all your hearts,*
> *Leaning not on our own understanding of circumstances*
> *In all our ways acknowledge Him*
> *And, then, then, then, and with great assurance, we will*

know that He directs our paths.

In the second church Roger pastored, I once attended a big event for pastor's wives where we were asked to share our thoughts about being a minister's wife. I, all too brightly, and not too wisely, raised my hand (I always hate to do that, but there I was, hand waving in the air.) I was called on, and said with great elegance and conviction, "God doesn't use a cookie cutter when it comes to ministers' wives." Everyone smiled and nodded. There was a smiling, good natured pause. Then a much *younger* pastor's wife raised her hand so she could add, all too sweetly I might add, that really, if we thought about it, our lives were all about being "servants." She really nailed that one.

> But, to be a servant you don't have to be a...
> Pianist
> Sunday school teacher,
> Youth worker,
> Vacation Bible school teachers.and most importantly,

we don't have to attend all the women's meetings.

> (Oh,thank you, Lord.)
> Amen.

Rather, we joyfully just have to be God's servants wherever he places us, just like every other Christian from day one. Our emphasis then becomes not, me, me, me; but Him, Him, Him, which becomes our life-long commitment to being a genuine follower of Christ.

Are there other biblical principles we can draw on for directing our steps as God's person and as pastor's wives? Many. We must search the scriptures. Of course, in our present hectic lifestyles, it's important to affirm that we can also be doctors, nurses, social workers, engineers, construction managers, or writers. All we do can be done as unto the Lord and for His glory. Remember the exquisite writer of Psalms succinctly makes it clear how to determine our paths.

The fear of the LORD is the beginning of wisdom;
all who follow his precepts have good understanding.
Psalm 111:10

Billy and Ruth Graham's daughter spoke at Ruth's funeral. She said with great elegance: "My mother's happiness and fulfillment did not depend on circumstances. She was the lovely, beautiful, wise woman she was because early in her life she chose Christ as her center, her home, her purpose, her partner, her confidante, her example and her vision. "

I must admit, there was great joy in not having the pressure of working outside of the home and, therefore, being available to nurture our children with time, and to come along side my husband at many events. It was great not having to deal with a nine to five demand, but to share life and ministry together. But not everyone can do that.

Chapter 46
ANGELS?

One Fall evening a few years ago while my husband was busily ministering at home, I was leaving my family's home in New Jersey, driving our five year old Audi the one with a sign on the license plate that read, "Please forgive me for having such a nice car. We got a great deal on it." It was dusk. I really shouldn't have started out on a twelve hour journey alone. I was about forty-five minutes on my way when all the warning lights on the dash flashed on...not a good sign I knew, like I was an MIT grad. I looked for a gas station. None. As well it began to dawn on me that I was in a city known as having one of the country's greatest crime rates. I had a sociology degree and had read about aggressive gangs and economic unrest in inner cities; plus I have a PhD in over-active imagination. (I was an honor student in that category.) Obviously, I had a decision to make, either have my car break down on the highway in the middle of the night on some forsaken road south, or venture off the next ramp into the ravages of the *Forbidden City*.

"Lord, please, please help me find a gas station and keep me safe." As I circled off the ramp, I finally saw a dimly lit gas station. (I must confess that not all of my prayers are answered that quickly.) *How come I hadn't seen that station before?* (That's one of those hmmm's) I experienced a great sense of relief, but at the same time realized that the station didn't have a repair garage. With no apparent other choices I pulled into the station, hoping someone would know what was wrong with my car. Before I got out of the car a young, handsome black man walked up to my window. Being my newly uncertain self, I opened the window just a crack and explained to the young man that all my dashboard warning lights had gone on.

"Open your hood; let me take a look." I obediently obeyed. After a long moment (my anxiety was in check) he walked back to my window and said, "Your serpentine belt, which runs the air conditioner, the generator and everything else, is broken and gone."

"What should I do?"

"Walk across the street to the truck stop and give him this number," (he seemed to know the number for the new belt, or was it a trap?), "and be careful cause truck stops are not too safe at night." It was now dark. Oh, why hadn't I left earlier? How come Roger doesn't take better care of our car! *Pity and anger come easily when you're scared.*

I said to the young man, "Are you an angel?" He smiled.

I wondered why he came to my window. There was no one else around that I could see. He didn't seem to be a worker at the gas station, nicely dressed actually, and I had just turned off the engine when he came to the window. And, now that I look back, he knew exactly what to do for my car. Who was he?

After looking both ways, just like Mom always said, I crossed the empty street, expecting to be jumped by some grizzly looking truck driver at any moment. (Now, how do you like my imagination?) But what I found was a polite man ready to help. He went inside the garage to see, I supposed, if he had the numbered belt, that his seeming friend across the street had written down. "Nope, sorry," he said as he returned, "I don't have that belt," I was crestfallen, "but give me a second and I'll call Pep Boys to see if they have one." Wow, every one was going the extra mile. He came back and said, "Go right away. Your car can easily limp its way there and Joe said he'd put the belt on for you and send you on your way. Hurry though, because they close in fifteen minutes." He gave me clear directions—just around the corner, turn left and at the light it's right there." He walked me to my car and opened the door and said, "God bless you, lady!"

A moment ago I was a frightened victim at a truck stop filled with dangerous goblins and demons, but then, a very helpful man who had solved my problem, walks me to my car and says, *"God bless you, Ma'am."*

He *was* an angel. Isn't it great the way God takes care of his children, even those with broken serpentine belts? I drove slowly and carefully around the corner. In fifteen minutes I was "On the road again."

God brings us serendipitous moments to encourage us and make us smile—even on desolate roads on our way home, and always when we minister to people who are frightened and are trying to find *their* way to their eternal home.

Something that I have found helpful is to keep letters and notes that people have written over the years telling of their triumphs and discouragements and how God has intervened or offered a caring hug during the tough and lost times. I can look back frequently to be reminded that, yes, God has used me to impact other lives for His Kingdom, and certainly and blessedly, God has used others to show me my way home.

If we seek His Kingdom and His righteousness, these things will be
added to us. Now, that's a promise.

Chapter 47
AN UNUSUAL ANNOUNCEMENT

Since my husband was pastor of the beautiful colonial styled First Presbyterian Church with a wonderful center isle and beautiful stain glass windows, I thought how nice it was that my daughter was at marrying age. Then the big phone call came from my daughter's boy friend asking her father's permission to marry Kathleen.

We were so excited and of course I mentally started decorating the church in my mind and making plans. Wrong! My daughter said, "Mom I've always wanted to get married outside in a beautiful park," and we did have beautiful parks in town. "Well honey, what if it rains?" And I thought secretly, "What would people think if the pastor's daughter didn't get married in the church. But a second better thought came: "God is also in the park".

I shifted gears and decided to do a beautiful "Martha Stewart" outside wedding with candles down the pathways leading to a circle of white pear trees that had enough space for white wooden chairs that could seat 250 people. There would be a beautifully decorated trellis that my artist brother could decorate perfectly and fresh flowers everywhere and a tree full of little vases with white candles hanging all over the tree that draped over the reception table. Perfect for an 8:30 p.m. wedding. My family and friends rallied to make these fantasies happen.

The morning started off with a wonderful and beautiful southern brunch in my friend's fairy tale like back yard for all the wedding party and out of town guests. It was perfect and so much fun being together for this happy occasion. The blue sky morning had everyone feeling pretty groovy. The afternoon found the wedding party swimming in a creek behind a plantation home, jumping out of a tree into Black Creek and eating a gourmet picnic hosted by other friends of the family. It was about at this time that things began to take a turn for the worse. The lovely shade of the Cyprus trees began to darken, and the guests began to glance at each other nervously. Someone talked about an afternoon rain shower coming, but this was fool's talk, and everybody knew it. A storm was a comin', and no man or woman on earth was going to stop it.

So at 8:00 p.m. we watched the rain pitter ever so pleasantly on our wedding chairs and tables and dance lightly inside the lanterns and glass candle holders hanging from every tree with their soggy little bows limply adorning their faces, and we were unhappy. News from the weather station was now filtering through the crowd "A tornado is coming." We now had thoughts of a sailor on a sinking ship. That was 8:00p.m. At 8:05 anyone who had been in the park was drenched and heading to the Church, at least we hoped. My daughter was sitting inside the church with frizzy little hair and a very sad face.

I thought to myself, "The important thing is the marriage of my daughter and Dan her fiancé." I tried to have the mind of Christ. I gave up the idea of a beautiful wedding. No flowers, no people, and no beautifully decorated reception. Then I heard the bagpipes begin and I began to think different sailor thoughts. Oh, at least we have the bagpipes playing.

I decided to look into the sanctuary from the bridal room at the back of the sanctuary while hair dryers were blowing in the back ground, to see if anyone had come through the storm to the church. The church platform was beautifully decorated with ferns and palms that had been dragged from the park by all our friends. The string quartet was in place but trying to get themselves and their instruments dried off. By the time the quartet started playing the wedding march, the church was almost full. The wedding started right on time!

"Oh Lord, you are so good! "

Unbeknown to me, my young mom's Bible study and my brother Paul skipped the wedding to decorate the fellowship hall for the reception. I had given up the idea of a reception. To move all the food, the wedding cake, silverware, drinks, table cloths, flowers etc. etc in forty minutes and decorate a whole room and set up with tables and chairs was Herculean, They did it! What a gift; what love. It almost made all the rain and winds worth it. I said almost.

Why do I tell this story? If you have a daughter who wants a wedding in a park or on the beach, or where ever she might come up with, remember God doesn't care where it is, because He will be there. But if you need help explaining why you might want it in the church you can use this story. Smile.

Chapter 48
DANGER—DON'T FALL

Sunday School, church, small group, Wednesday night dinner, committee meetings, family camp, marriage and family retreats, missions emphases week, spiritual emphases week, women's Bible studies, prayer meeting....... Over eating makes you sick and the added pounds makes you sluggish and you don't desire to walk let alone run.

What can happen physically can also happen in the spiritual realm especially to minister's wives if we are not careful. We often, to be with our husbands, have to attend many more events than most of the congregation, so over eating spiritually can definitely be a danger.

How do we prevent the above and other spiritual downfalls? Of course it is a very individual matter, but here are a few things I have found helpful.

Taking in, and taking in without giving out, causes spiritual constipation. Bring along a non-Christian or a young, struggling Christian to some of your meetings and you begin to hear the talks in a new fresh way. It picks up your prayer life also.

When you are having your personal time with God and in His Word make sure you take what you have read and specifically apply it to your life that day or week, and pray for God's empowering with those issues. Write it down and check on yourself. The simple three steps I often use and you have heard many times are:

What does the Bible passage say?

What does it mean?

What does it mean to me? This personalizing is the most important part, since obeying is what it is all about.

What am I going to do about it?

"Do not merely listen to the word and so deceive yourselves. Do what it says." James 1:22

Find a good friend that can hold you accountable for those areas in your life you are struggling with or working on. It doesn't have to be a meeting, but a phone call, or a luncheon date where you can be totally honest and where you can be uplifted.

As iron sharpens iron, so one man sharpens another. Proverbs 27:17

Get out of the Christian Ghetto! Instead, try the teachers lounge, the country club, the Newcomers Cub, a book club, the P.T.A., work for Habitat for Humanity, or the Hospital. These places mentioned begin to give us opportunity to use some of that knowledge we have been collecting with out having to regurgitate. Please don't choose them all.

"All authority in heaven and on earth has been given to me, therefore go and make disciples of all nations..." Matthew 28:19.

In one of my Education Psychology courses they recommended always studying in the same quiet, uncluttered, without distractions place, so that psychologically when you go to that place, your mind automatically is ready to study. I believe this principle works with our time with the Lord, a place that for you where it is easy to tune your heart to the Lord. Being an aesthetic person, creation can greatly stimulate my worship, so I sit at a table with a window looking out to the woods and the array of colorful birds to trigger praise and thankfulness. It always brings forth praise. I also have my Bible and note book to write down what God has been showing me in my reading. Each of us is different, but I recommend trying different things until they work for you.

Prayer is a hard one for me. I can't go through lists day after day because I know that He heard me the first time, but then I am reminded of the woman who kept pounding on the door and was finally heard because of her pounding.

Two things seem to work with me: Kneeling. It reminds me that I am talking to the almighty King and also it reminds me that I am praying. The other is walking outside as I pray. What works for you?

I had a Christian friend at one time whose father was the ambassador to Greece. One day the son was coming out of the embassy to catch a cab. As he was in the cab, my friend thought to himself. I wonder if the driver knew that I was just eating dinner sitting near the King of Greece, what he would think. He surely would be impressed. Then in a flash the thought came to him. I come before the King of Kings and Lord of Lords every day and I treat it like it is nothing. That story always helps me get perspective on prayer quickly.

Small couples' groups have been one of the best places for spiritual growth for my husband and me. To be able to share our lives with a caring group is priceless. A small group can be a place where we hear people praying for our needs and we pray for theirs. When we report back what God has done in answer to our prayers, it is faith building. A small group can become a place where you can discuss the Word of God and together figure out how it applies to your lives. They can also be a safe place to raise questions and a place where you see God change lives before your very eyes. Now a group like that takes time to develop, so hang in there for the trust level to grow. And as a pastor and his wife, when the group sees you on the same journey they are on, it frees them to be honest and begin to grow.

Getting off alone with your husband to a specialized conference for pastors and wives has been so helpful, because you do have specific needs that lay people don't. It helps me be able to laugh at similar situations that other pastors and their wives share and to be able to ask questions. Plus you are not looked to as the leader in this setting, so it feels very relaxed. Above all those reasons, the spiritual encouragement and teaching is usually aimed right at your needs.

Choose to read books that will challenge you in the areas where you are struggling. Those challenges definitely change with the different stages of your life.

When you have babies, it is another ball game. Billy Graham's wife said she was so busy with her children, she put her Bible on her kitchen counter and as she went by it she would read a verse and meditate on it as she ran through her day. Susanna Wesley told her many children that when she had her apron pulled over her head, she was talking to God and they were not to bother her.

Books that challenge me are missionary biographies. They always help me put my life into perspective. I believe there is a good book for every struggle we might have, every stage in life that we are in and any question we might have. If you are not a big reader, use audio books. There's incredible stuff out there to teach us and encourage us. One book that helped me put my life into perspective was: <u>Missionary Patriarch</u>, the story of John Paton and his work among the South Seas Cannibals. It was also very interesting to read his wife's account of the same experiences in her book, <u>Margaret Paton, Letters from the South Seas</u>. Seeing how a husband and wife looked at the same experiences so very differently was quite helpful.

Another spiritual encouragement for me has been discovering my spiritual gift and using it instead of trying to do everything. Of course, God can use us in our weakness as well, but I mainly try to do those things that bring me joy because they are what God created me to do.

Basically the four elements that need to be a part of spiritual growth are

FELLOWSHIP, INSTRUCTION, WORSHIP, SERVICE

They devoted themselves to the *apostles teaching* (instruction), and to the (*fellowship*), to the *breaking of bread, and to prayer* (worship). Acts 2: 42 *Selling their possessions and goods they gave to anyone as he had need.* (service) Acts 2:45

It is important that we keep these four elements of ministry in balance.

Now to him who is able to do immeasurably more than all we ask or imagine, according to his power that is at work within us, to him be glory in the church and in Christ Jesus throughout all generations for ever and ever! Amen. Jude 24-25.

Chapter 49
THE KEY

Our husbands preach and teach life changing truths. They preserve and proclaim biblical imperatives. Their congregations and our wider communities need their voices *crying in the wilderness,* and shouting to our city's growing multitudes: "Make straight the path of the Lord."

Even with all their crying and shouting, it is easy for those of us, their *helpmates,* to become ho-hum about our husband's ministries. Too often we forget to pray for our husbands that they will have increasing wisdom and spiritual empowering.

What follows is a list of helpful Bible passages from Thessalonians and the Pastoral Epistles that relate to prayer for those in ministry.   Study and meditate upon two or three verses each day. Then pray those verses for your husband.

1. I Thes. 2:2-4
Pray they will speak as messengers from God, trusted by him to tell the truth; pray they will change His message not one bit to suit the taste of those who hear it. For we serve God alone.

2. I Thes. 2:5
Pray they will not be friends just to receive things or money.

3. I Thes. 2:12
Pray that their daily lives will not embarrass God.

4. II Tim. 4:4
Pray they will correct and rebuke their people when they need it and encourage them to do right.

5. I Thes. 3:1-3
Pray they will be an encourager of the faith to their people.

6. I Thes. 4:1, 2
Pray they will live lives more closely to the ideal (pure, free from sexual sin).

7. I Tim. 1:5
Pray they will love the brethren more and more.

8. II Thes. 3:1
Pray that the Lord's message will spread rapidly and triumphantly wherever it goes, winning people to Christ everywhere.

9. I Tim. 11:5
Pray for pure hearts, clean minds, and a strong faith.

10. I Tim. 1:12
Pray for strength for your husband to be faithful to God in every area.

11. I Tim. 2:1
Pray that they would become men of prayer for others.

12. I Tim. 3:1
Pray that they will be good men whose lives cannot be spoken against.

13. I Tim. 3:2
Pray they will be hard workers, thoughtful, orderly, and full of good deeds.

14. I Tim. 3:2
Pray that they will enjoy having guests in their homes and be good Bible teachers

15. I Tim. 3:3
Pray they will not be addicted to wine, not quarrelsome, but gentle and kind.

16. I Tim. 3:4
Pray they manage their own households well, keeping them under control with all dignity.

17. I Tim. 3:6
Pray they will keep from pride.

18. I Tim. 4:7
Pray they will discipline themselves for the purpose of godliness.

19. I Tim. 4:14
Pray they will use well the abilities God gave them..

20. I Tim. 5:1
Pray that they will respect older men.

21. I Tim. 5:4
Pray that their kindness will begin at home.

22. I Tim. 6:14
Pray they will fulfill all He has told them to do so no one can find fault.

23. I Tim. 6:17
Pray they will not trust in the uncertainty of riches.

24. I Tim. 6:20
Pray they will keep out of foolish arguments with those who boast of their knowledge.

25. II Tim. 1:13
Pray they will retain the standard of sound words which they have heard from the scriptures, especially concerning the faith and love that Christ Jesus offers them.

26. II Tim. 2:1
Pray that they would be strong with the strength Christ Jesus gives them. For they must teach others those things they have heard me speak about.

27. II Tim. 2:2
Pray that they will teach God's truth to trustworthy men, who will pass them on to others

28. II Tim. 2:3
Pray that they will be able to take their share of suffering as soldiers of Jesus Christ

29. II Tim. 2:3
Pray that they won't get caught up in worldly affairs.

30. II Tim. 2:5
Pray that they will follow the Lord's rules for doing His work.

31. II Tim. 2:6
Pray that they will work hard like a farmer.

32. II Tim. 2:14
Pray that they won't argue over unimportant things. Such arguments are confusing, useless, and even hurtful.

33. II Tim. 3:15
Pray that they would know what His word says and means

34. II Tim 4:2
Pray they will be humble toward those who are mixed up about their faith because:
a. They will be more likely to turn back to God.
b. They will more likely come to their senses."

35. II Tim. 4:2
Pray they will preach the Word of God urgently at all times, whenever they get the chance.

36. II Tim 4:4
Pray they will correct and rebuke their people when they need it and encourage them to do right.

About the Author

Joy Keating Gulick has been a pastor's wife for over 40 years, in four different churches. She lived most of her growing up years in the Northeast, and most of her married life in the Southeast. Joy is a graduate of Wheaton College, and did graduate studies in Christian Education. Before marriage she worked for Young Life in Baltimore, Maryland for three years, and taught school for two years in New Hampshire and California. Joy and her husband, Roger, now live on Lookout Mountain, Georgia above Chattanooga. In semi-retirement they are pastoring missionaries all over the world with a mission called Entrust.

11980446R00103

Made in the USA
Charleston, SC
02 April 2012